1804~
THAT WAS THE YEAR...

1804 ~
THAT WAS THE YEAR...

Compiled by

Sheila M. Hardy

Illustrated by
Anne Fletcher

BRECHINSET PUBLICATIONS
7-11 King Street, Ipswich, Suffolk, England IP1 1EG

ISBN 0—947681—05—1

© Sheila Hardy 1984

Designed and typeset by Brechinset Publications, Ipswich
Printed and bound by The Garden City Press Limited, Letchworth

Contents

To Michael, Damyon and Robert,
and all those who have had to put up with
my enthusiasm for the year 1804

Acknowledgements

My sincere thanks to the Suffolk Records Office for permission to use the material from the Ipswich Journal, and to all the staff for their friendly interest and help.

To Lord Coke, and Mr. F. C. Jolly the Administrator of Holkham Estate for their help in verifying information.

In reproducing the extracts contained in this publication, the original layout, spelling and punctuation have been maintained wherever possible.

Introduction

Old newspapers always make fascinating reading: last week's copy of an unfamiliar 'Sunday' wrapped round the potatoes can delay preparations for lunch for several minutes, and the sheets which lined the bottom of a chest of drawers will certainly stop the ruthless spring cleaner for at least half-an-hour with recollections of what was happening in the world last year, causing gasps of wonder at the price of cars or houses, or at the salaries offered in the Sits. Vac. column. Go back ten or twenty years and one becomes conscious of how 'old fashioned' everything from the style of the journalism to the tone of the advertisements seems. To go back one hundred and eighty years, to go back into History, might be amusing, might even be enlightening, if one is interested in the past, but is there really anything to be gained from looking at a set of newspapers from the 1800s?

The Suffolk Records Office, which is in constant use by researchers of all kinds, decided that a comprehensive index of all the old newspapers in the Archives would be of great value, so that future researchers would know exactly where to go for particular information about the County. The brief given to the small band of volunteer Indexers of the Ipswich Journals from 1800 onwards, was simple — read through each week's copy of the four page newspaper and extract all relevant material. This way, it was hoped, a picture of life would be built up; which trades and occupations were carried on in the towns and villages; what type of case came to court and how severe were the sentences; how did the population of the time in Suffolk fit in with the generally known history of the period. Bearing in mind the current interest in genealogy, the obituary columns came in for very close scrutiny, and while establishing dates and places of residence for the use of Family Tree collectors, it was often possible also to identify epidemics or sad cases of premature death from diseases such as Consumption.

The Ipswich Journal, like many other papers of the period, was a double sheet, similar in size to today's Daily Telegraph.

Each of the four sides was divided into five columns. Unlike our modern newspapers, there were no headlines for stories, and one could not skim across the front page to pick out the major items. Amongst the close type it was easy to miss some important item, so close reading was required. The Indexers were to read the columns on page two which were headed 'Ipswich Today' and go through the various advertisements and announcements which appeared throughout the Journal. This was a time consuming, albeit fascinating, operation, particularly if one strayed into the news from London and elsewhere which appeared on pages one, two and four under the heading of Sunday's, Wednesday's and Friday's Post, for here were the titbits of history which made one's old school history book much more alive. One found oneself looking at Napoleon through the eyes of his contemporaries rather than with twentieth century hindsight, and the rather smug amusement I had experienced when reading of the invasion alarms in such novels as *The Trumpet Major* and *Cranford* turned to a genuine concern when I read of French frigates coming close in shore at Brighton and capturing British ships.

In his introduction to *The Trumpet Major*, Thomas Hardy states that he owed much to the newspapers of the period to provide background to his story; just how much he had relied on them became more obvious as I combed through my papers — at times I felt I was reading the novel, and when I went back to the novel, I was able to identify whole passages which were based on actual happenings. It was this aspect, of making the literature of the period come so alive, that first led me to collecting some of the items which follow. I found it exciting to re-read novels, plays and poems of the period with a far greater understanding of the mood of the time. Minor details which would have been glossed over, now had meaning — for example, the play which caused so much concern in Jane Austen's *Mansfield Park* proved to be one of those in which the 'pop' actor of 1804 appeared. And what an eye opener too were the enormous fees he commanded.

Carefully recording the sentence meted out at the Assizes

held in January for abduction (a crime which was to occur very commonly thus making me realise that Jane Austen was relating actual happenings) my attention was drawn to the name of the accused. It was one I knew well. I scoured the columns of the previous year to see if I could find a reference to the man's first being charged, for it was essential I should find out where he lived. My quest was in vain, but it is both tempting and amusing to speculate that the cottage at Flatford Mill immortalised by John Constable might once have been a love nest. However, when presented with facts one tries hard not to make assumptions and no doubt it was pure coincidence that the Romeo brought to justice was called Willie Lott.

The more I read, the more I became aware of the similarities between 1804 and the present. It would be invidious to point to actual cases, but I hope that as you read what follows, you too will find the parallels that can be made in politics, criminal activities and in general attitudes. It was a period of uncertainty, a time of rising prices, high unemployment, social unrest and violence. Yet in an age when republicanism flourished elsewhere, the Royal Family's popularity was high and their every move was watched and reported on with keen interest. No one forced the populace to wait hours on end for a brief glimpse of the king's coach as did the occupants of Overcombe Mill in *The Trumpet Major,* yet the newspapers report that they did.

And in an era in which feminism has flourished, how strange it was to read that nearly two hundred years ago ladies campaigned against the itinerant sellers of obscene prints which were thought to pervert the young — shades of twentieth century pornographic magazines and video 'nasties'. It was also accepted practice for a widow to take over the running of her husband's business; women shoeworkers went on strike after the men had settled their pay claim, and it was even possible for a woman of humble origins to sue her employer in court for unfair dismissal.

The year 1804 held many surprises for me, and I hope that you will enjoy reading some of the curious, comic and cautionary stories of yesteryear which prove without doubt that human nature changes very little.

Entertainments

In the 1940s and 50s, most entertainment was derived from the cinema. For those who did not sneak in as the doors opened just after lunch to stay until the National Anthem was played around 10.30, a visit to the Pictures meant a good three hours entertainment. For a modest 1/9 (under 10p) one would get, and expect to get, two films, the 'big picture' with a star cast, and a slightly shorter, less expensively made one. But that was not all, apart from the newsreels and the advertisements, there would be some other diversion, possibly a series of cartoons, or, in certain cinemas, the mighty Wurlitzer organ would rise majestically from the bowels of the earth to cause wonder and delight to the children not only from the noise it produced, but also by the magical way the lights inside the organ casing could change colour.

To get into the cinema, one invariably had to queue, which one did with that traditional British sense of fair play and fair shares for all. Quite when this became traditional, I don't know, but it certainly was not part of the late 18th and early 19th century way of life, as you will see in the descriptions of the scrums which took place at the London theatres when the 'idol' of the day appeared.

The programmes at the theatres of 1804 bear a strong similarity to those old days of the cinema; there would be a full length play of five acts, plus a short farce, and for the interval between, some form of entertainment such as juggling, acrobatics, tight-rope walking or a song and dance routine, items which later in the century were to develop into a separate form of entertainment known as the Musical Hall or Variety Theatre: — a separation which has perhaps done untold damage to the theatre-going public. Nearly two hundred years ago, the average playgoer would happily sit through a performance of Shakespeare's plays, often offering advice to an actor in a way seen nowadays only at the pantomime, and enjoy it every bit as much as he did the light-hearted farces which poked fun at his everyday life. A play was a play — not 'Literature' and therefore to be avoided at all costs.

Most provincial theatres today have to rely heavily on subsidies in order to keep going. Ipswich has an excellent new theatre, but its patrons are well aware that their ticket money alone will not pay for the production, that sponsorship will have to come from one or other of the local firms. Again, this is not new, this isn't a state of affairs brought about by governments determined to deny us pleasure, the Ipswich theatre of 1804, like all the theatres around the country (and even very small towns had a theatre) had to rely on financial backing from some source or other, perhaps the Officers quartered in the town, the local Masonic Lodges or the owners of the many small and select Academies for Young Ladies and Gentlemen.

If you wanted other entertainment and you were not one of those invited to the large fancy dress balls of the wealthy, then you could always stand by the entrance of the mansion where it was being held and look at the costumes of the dancers. Or you might attend one of the many provincial assemblies or dances which were held on the flimsiest of excuses — Ipswich people turned out to celebrate the birthday of the King of Prussia. With a large number of military men in the town, the daughters of tradesmen and farmers were always sure of a partner.

There were musical societies and concerts for those who were that way inclined, philosophical lectures for those with a serious turn of mind, and for the curious there might be a travelling show which exhibited a human being with some form of physical abnormality. Behind closed doors there was gambling galore, for vast fortunes dependent on the turn of a card or the throw of a die (whist occupied many of Ipswich's leading citizens) or for smaller sums at the cockfights or barefisted boxing bouts.

For those desiring more sedentary pleasure, then what better than a cosy chat over the tea-cups exchanging news of the activities and fashions of the Royal Family. What was the Princess of Wales, that great fashion setter appearing in this week, who had the Prince of Wales taken to Brighton, which wealthy young lady had eloped with a penniless officer, or worse still, her father's coachman. Strange marriages were discussed, those where age differences almost certainly betokened an interest in the older party's financial rather than physical assets. And strange to us now does it seem to read of a wedding taking place late at night, not in a church but in a fashionable London mansion, with a banquet preceding the marriage service not after it. Our traditional wedding, is we find, not quite as old as we had thought.

And while we may marvel at finding that some things are not as old as we thought, let us stop to consider those which turn out to be much older than we would have believed possible. The 'Media' so we are constantly being told, is responsible for shaping our thoughts about certain topics. We have all witnessed the making or breaking of a career or reputation by over-exposure in newspapers and on T.V. and radio. That such a thing could happen nearly two hundred years ago seems unbelievable, after all, look how long it took for news to travel — one of Nelson's famous sea battles could have been over and done with nearly a month before the details reached London. Yet within the United Kingdom, news could, and did, travel fast, and with the right publicity, reputations could be built up and destroyed. The near hysteria which greeted young William Betty when he finally made his London debut is paralleled by that which accompanies so many of today's 'Pop' stars, yet there are those who would have us believe that 'it wasn't like this in the old days'.

The Power of Advertising

"Whatever did they do before they had television?" is a question which can apply as much to advertising as to the dissemination of news or the provision of entertainment. Our children learn to sing advertising jingles before nursery rhymes, and many a mother has been heard to remark wryly, on hearing her older offspring repeat, word perfect, the dialogue which occurs in a T.V. advertisement, that she wished that they could apply the same concentration to their school work.

Today, like it or not, if we are television viewers, then we are subjected to advertising in various forms. Companies spend a vast amount of time and energy, not to mention money, in finding the right psychological and sociological methods to persuade us to buy products we don't really need, so that we may create an image of ourselves as kind and loving, strong and virile, or beautiful and feminine; alternatively it may be that we are urged to keep up with, or better still, overtake our neighbours, by owning the very latest in . . . whatever it is.

To safeguard us from the harm that might befall those who are too gullible, a code of acceptable standards for advertising has been drawn up. Products are no longer allowed to have claims made on their behalf which cannot be substantiated, like the miraculous nature of a certain well known washing powder, which in the late 1950s had a member of the public misreading her cue card and announcing to the world at large that Brand X "is very good. I find I've got three children . . ."

It was probably gaffes such as this which led to the use of professional actors to endorse products, thus giving us the pleasure of seeing our favourite players in sophisticated advertisements which not only amuse us, but make us reason that the product must be good if so and so says it is.

What, you may ask, has all this to do with 1804. A great deal, since advertising made up a very large part of the newspapers of the period, and following my hypothesis that nothing is new, we find when we look at the advertisements in the Ipswich Journal, that many of them follow exactly the same line of reasoning as those of today. Although no doubt Fanny Kemble's endorsement of Lupin soap would have carried some weight, it was obviously much better if one could appeal to the snob which is in all of us, and so the aristocracy were called upon to lend their names to such important products as Ching's Patent Worm Powders. If the Duchess Downtown and the Bishop of Blankshire said they were efficacious, then who among the lower orders would dare to question?

What is most interesting about the advertisements of the early nineteenth century is their emphasis on health. Disease of the bowel, we are told, is the scourge of the twentieth century western world. Too much refined food, not enough dietary fibre, too many chemical additives . . . Look carefully at the advertisements which follow and you will see numerous remedies for constipation, biliousness, indigestion, worms, pimples and bad breath. With their tremendous concern for inner cleanliness, it is not surprising that foreigners accused the English of being obsessed with their bowels.

We can learn too, something of the other diseases which were then prevalent and are still with us. You may be surprised at the outspoken manner of expression in some of the advertisements. Certain topics have but recently found mention in today's press; one advertisement, which by our present day standards is very explicit, states that delicacy forbids it from mentioning further details!

Another surprise is the vast number of books which were published at this time, especially as we tend to think that literacy is the prerogative of the twentieth century. But education was available to those whose parents could afford the quite moderate fees, and for those who could not, there were several manuals of the 'Teach Yourself' variety.

Much can be learnt of the manners and morals of an age from studying its advertisements. We read of the 'Lady Bountiful' who ordered large quantities of chilblain remedies with which to treat the poor of her district, of the poor girl who would lose her job if she did not have another bottle of cough mixture to keep her able to work. The more one reads of the period, the more one questions what was it that caused the depression, melancholia and madness that so many suffered from. Was it the excessive use of mercury and other chemicals? In the same way that we now question the overprescription of drugs and the use of additives in our processed foods, so too did the people of 1804 ask about their treatments.

Other advertisements, the small ones for jobs, houses, articles for sale and so on, bear a striking similarity to those of today. Carriages cost just as much as the modern prestigious car, tenants seeking furnished accommodation are careful to point out they are childless. Advertisers then, as now, paid for their advertisements by the line, with a special rate for second and subsequent insertions. The only difference, and perhaps I ought not to mention it, in case the Chancellor should get to hear of it, was that in the early nineteenth century a duty was payable on all advertisements, and it was the editor's responsibility to have the money ready for the Inspector and Collector of Duty thirty days after the advertisement first appeared. Thus, every editor printed in his paper the fact that 'ready money should accompany each advertisement.'

Is this a Record?

Lately died in Ireland, Roger Byrne, the famous Irish Giant. He is said to have died of suffocation, occasioned by an extremity of fat, which stopped the play of his lungs and put a period to his life in the fifty fourth year of his age. His coffin, with its contents, weighed 52 stones; it was borne on a very long bier by 30 men, who were relieved at intervals. He was 13 stone heavier than the noted Bright of Maldon, whose waistcoat inclosed seven persons.

Mr. Haugh, living at Stanwix, near Carlisle, is in possession of a thrush which has excited the admiration of some hundreds of persons. The bird (brought up from the nest) he has kept in a cage upwards of eight years; and it is remarkable both for feather and song, and has never pined beneath either hurt or sickness, yet it has gradually obtained a complete regeneration of its legs and feet. About the close of the seventh year, these members gave signs of decay; when from each thigh there appeared to issue two bones, like two slender pipes cemented together, and as the old legs and feet on the one side shrunk and diminished the new ones protruded on the other, daily acquiring strength and activity.

On the evening of 1, June, a skaite of very uncommon size was caught in a salmon net, at the Point of Fortrose, Rosshire. It measured from the tip of the nose to the point of the tail 6'6" and its extreme breadth 5'8". It was proportionally thick, and required four men to carry it from the shore.

Lately died at Lithuania in Poland, a man at the great age of 168.

A Lycoperdon, or Puff-ball, of a most extraordinary size, has recently been gathered at Horsecroft; it is of a globular form and measures 4'7" in circumference.

Thursday week there fell on Old Malon Moor, the most extraordinary shower of hail ever remembered in that part of the country, attended with heavy rolls of thunder, and flashes of lightning extremely vivid. The hailstones were as large as marbles, and the impetuosity so great, that in less than two minutes the ground was covered upwards of 4" thick, and every field of corn within its sweep almost destroyed; and some fields of wheat so completely, that the proprietors have determined on ploughing them out to avail themselves of the season for turnips.

A lady in Leeds of 52 gave birth to a daughter; her last child is now in her twenty eighth year.

On the 8th.inst.was cut by Mr. Griffin, gardener to I.C. Giradot, Esq. of Kelham, nr. Newark, a pineapple, of the new Providence kind, which weighed 9lbs 3oz, and in July last one was cut weighing 7lbs. 2oz. The above plants produced fruit when two years old.

Mr. Samuel Lambert, Master of the County Gaol of Leicester, is supposed to be the heaviest man in the kingdom, being of the enormous weight of 46 stones 12 lbs.

Lately died at Gloves, near Athenry, Ireland, after a short illness, Mr. Dennis Corrobee of Ballindangin, aged 117, a truly honest man. He retained his faculties to the last, and until 2 days previous to his death, he never remembered to have any complaints or sickness whatever, (toothache only excepted.) He could, to the last, read the smallest print without the assistance of glasses. It has been acknowledged that, for the present age, he was the most experienced farmer, and the brightest genius for the improvement of agriculture; it is upwards of 70 years since he propagated that most useful article to the human species, called the black potatoe. He was married 7 times and when married to the last he was 93; by them all he had 48 children, 236 grandchildren, 944 great grandchildren, and 25 great, great grandchildren, the eldest of whom is 4 years, and his own youngest son (by his last wife) is about 18.

An extraordinary circumstance was lately mentioned of the death of a woman at Cadoxstone, when her mother, 70 years of age, took the infant of her deceased daughter, and placing it at her own breast received an immediate supply of milk for its support. The singularity of this event caused many inquiries; and a gentleman in the neighbourhood, of the highest respectability, has come forward and affirmed that the woman's age is 72; and that the infant thrives very fast and that the milk is as fine as that of a young woman.

A famous Leicester hog, slaughtered by Mr. Gittin of Bridnorth, though remarkably small in bone weighed 651 lbs and his inside fat 83 lbs.

There is a person of the name of Stephen Sharp, a farmer, late of Knaresboro' and is at present an inhabitant of Bramhope, near Otley, who has attained the extraordinary age of 106.

Mrs. Joyce, wife of Mr. Joyce of the King's Head, Bocking, was recently delivered of a son and daughter, being the fourth time she has brought forth twins.

Aged 91, has died, Mr. Edward Ward, gardener. He had not wholly ceased to work in the garden till his last illness, about five weeks before his death, when he was confined to his bed by a total debility. Till he was turned 87 he could not be said to be infirm, as he retained all his faculties. He had been from his childhood in Mr. Lofft's family, and reckoning lineally from parent to child the Wards had been employed in that family for near 200 years.

On Tuesday last there was the lowest tide that has ever been known within the memory of man in the river Thames.

Some gooseberries were pulled in a garden of Mr. Allen of Hill-Head, near Ravensworth, three of which measured 4" in circumference and one weighed 8 dwts 12 gr.

At St. Matthew's Workhouse, the wives of two corporals in the Militia were both delivered of twins on the same day.

A few days since a woman of the name of Ligo, 58 years of age, living in Bethnal Green was delivered of a male child, who with the mother is in a fair way. Two days after, her grand daughter was delivered of twins. What renders this circumstance the more extraordinary is, that the old lady had not had a child since she was thirty two years of age.

Foreign News

On the 20, May, Bonaparte was formally proclaimed Emperor with great parade. It is a curious fact, that the actual duration of the Republic of France has been so long only as just to equal the duration of the Commonwealth in England which was 11 years and 4 months to a day, if the commencement of both be dated from the death of the Kings.

The new Nizam is building a magnificent palace some miles from Hyderabad. His Zanana, which is charmingly situated on the banks of the river, is to be competent to the accommodation of *three thousand of his wives.*

The Dutch are esteemed the most thrifty of any people in Europe; and the most easily contented with coarse plain fare. Yet, at the Cape of Good Hope, they knew not the use of sheep's head, tripe, or cow-heel, till that was taught them by our soldiers, Scotch and English when the Cape was lately in British possession.

A tornado of the most violent kind occurred at George Town and Flemington, on the Potomack, America on 22 May. It began in the evening, after a very sultry day and was preceded by a slight shower, which lasted about an hour; after which a black cloud overspread the horizon; a column of thick black vapour also arose from the earth to the height of 40', and resembled a waterspout; it was attended with a noise like thunder, and it was generally supposed that an earthquake was approaching. A total darkness prevailed within the vortex of the whirlwind; it proceeded through the middle of the village of Flemington, carrying away every light building etc., particularly a stable 60' in length. Most of the dwelling houses were uprooted, chimnies blown down, and some furniture conveyed out of the windows to a considerable distance. After passing through a wood to the east of the village, in which it tore up some of the largest trees by the roots, it was observed to break against a hill and the vapour to disperse in a moment.

Bremen, after a blockade of 5 weeks by the Corsican's Satellites, during the present uninterrupted Continental peace, has, at last, been forced to advance a loan, or rather submit to a requisition of one million dollars, necessary for the mock Emperor's Coronation expences. Bonaparte, report says, has caused the most tempting offers of lucrative public offices etc. to be made to some rich Jews to leave England and reside in France; but the Moneyers are not to be outwitted in such a way by the crafty Corsican.

Lt. Bowen sailed from Sidney, New South Wales in June, 1803, with the rank of Lieutenant Governor to form a new settlement on Van Diemen's Land . . . a number of convicts, guilty of recent petty crimes are to be sent . . . among them the unfortunate Sir Henry Hays. He incurs this punishment in consequence of having founded a lodge of Free Masons in opposition to the orders of Governor King.

Pullean, an instrument-maker, at Moskow, has invented a curious musical instrument, called Orchestrino, which has been heard in the different theatres in Russia, with great applause. It has the same effect upon the audience as a well composed orchestra of 400 select musicians. He has obtained from the Emperor of Russia an exclusive privilege for ten years, and intends to travel with it and visit the principal towns and cities of Europe.

It is said that Bonaparte wrote a very indignant letter to Mr. Jefferson, President of the United States which reproached the latter in very severe terms for having suffered his brother Jerome to degrade himself by marrying the daughter of a private American citizen. Now this self-same Jerome was, a few years ago, in a menial capacity at Lyons; and the Lady he has married, is one of the prettiest women in America, with a fortune of 50,000 dollars.

The famous aeronaut Blanchard is now at Marseilles. His balloon is of that extent, that it can, without danger, ascend with 9 persons, not heavier than himself; which was proved on 6, July when four young ladies and four young gentlemen ascended with him and danced a quadrille in the air, 1500' from the earth.

Paris Papers to the 21 July, contain ample details of the pomp and pageantry of the *Imperial* family in the Fete of the 14 July. The good people of Paris seem quite delighted with the magnificent establishment of their *august* Head; and he, knowing the character of the people with whom he has to deal, seems determined that they have abundance of show to console them for the loss of that liberty for which they have been contending for twelve years.

Abbe Sicard, the humane Inspector of the Deaf and Dumb, whose zeal and talents have penetrated into Russia, has received from the Russian Emperor and Empress, two beautiful diamond rings of great value.

An architect of the Prince of Lichenstein has discovered a method of making bricks and tiles without the co-operation of fire; and the article manufactured is strong enough to be

preserved entire beneath the most violent strokes of the
hammer. He has prepared them to every shape and consistence,
and they are either suited to subterraneous works, to roofings
or to the walls of buildings.

Bonaparte and his Empress, during their journey in the con-
quered departments made use of no other bedstead, but one of
iron, carried with them, of the invention of Mr. Sanecy in the
Rue St. Antoine. In two minutes this bed may be set up and
taken down, and its whole weight is only 7 lbs. The mechanism
is so ingenious that it may easily be taken to pieces in five
minutes, and requires no more space than an usual travelling
trunk to contain it.

It is stated as an article of intelligence from Italy, that Malta is
to be given up to Russia.

150 Dutch fishermen now fish under Prussian colours, un-
molested by the English.

Advantage seems to have been taken of the late hurricane to raise the price of every article of West Indian produce. Sugar rose 12%, coffee 5%. There was little or no alteration in the price of cotton.

An English Gentleman left Alicante on the 16 Sept. on board a Danish vessel, after having had the yellow fever. They touched at Gibraltar on 2 Oct., but were not allowed to enter the port. The fever had seized the garrison and between 50 and 60 were dying daily. The Gentleman left the Danish vessel, and landed in an open boat between Brighton and Worthing and appeared on Monday upon the Exchange. This proceeding, so contrary to the laws against the breach of quarantine, have subjected him to penalties of the law, and we understand he was on Tuesday put under arrest. The alarm in Gibraltar was very great. It is said that a rich Jew offered the master of a vessel 700£ to carry him and his family away, and all who can quit the place. Many, it is said, have betaken themselves to living in any sort of craft on the water to be out of the way of the infection.

General Lake has obtained 52,000£ as his share of the spoil in one of his Asiatic conquests.

It is stated to have been agreed, between England and Russia, that Malta shall be occupied by them conjointly, in consequence of which 5,000 Russian troops are now on their voyage for that island.

Louis XVIII has been received at Calais with all the honours due to a crowned head. Illuminations, firings of cannons etc. took place on the occasion. The Swedish Governor of the Province complimented His Majesty on his arrival.

Sir George Rumbold, our Minister at Hamburgh, has been carried off by a body of French Troops! Sir George was at his country seat near Hamburgh. A body of French Troops crossed the Elbe and landed between Altona and Hamburgh on the 24th,ult. at night, and without any notice or communication to the Senate of Hamburgh, carried him a close prisoner to Harburgh, from whence, probably he will be sent to Paris and imprisoned in the Temple! Sir George hearing a noise, looked out at the window, and seeing the house surrounded by soldiers, asked what they wanted; they told him they had some dispatches for him; but he refusing to suffer the door to be opened, they forced it open, and carried him away by force, having first obliged him to deliver up to them all his papers. The Senate was in consequence assembled from 7 o'clock in the morning till 5 in the evening; they sent a deputation to the French Ministry, to protest against this violation of their territory, and demanded that the English Charge d'Affaires should be set at liberty. The French Ministry, it is said, denies having any knowledge of the transaction. Couriers have also been sent off to Berlin, Vienna and Petersburgh. Sir George has been carried to Hanover in a coach, under a strong escort.

Various opinions have at different times prevailed, respecting the time and weather when Bonaparte will actually invade us. To these we shall add that of an American Correspondent. He says, that the important descent will take place, when it is so windy as to blow the British Squadron from the French coast, and yet so calm as to enable French gun boats to row across the Channel; when it is so light that Frenchmen shall see their way, and yet so dark as to prevent Englishmen from seeing them!

Letter from Bonaparte addressed to Burgomaster and Council of City of Frankfurt — 1 Oct. 1804.
"Very Worthy and Good Friends . . .
I shall always perceive with pleasure, that you take such

measures as may prevent your city from becoming the centre of those intrigues and disturbances which England endeavours to propagate on the continent to mislead it, and renew the evils of war, the calamities of which you have already sufficiently experienced. . . ."

It was confidently rumoured, yesterday morning, that war with Spain has become inevitable.

The Pope will leave Rome for Paris on Nov. 3rd, accompanied by five Cardinals, four Bishops and other ecclesiastics. The number of persons who will accompany him exceeds eighty.

A letter from General Wellesley's camp, dated 6, June, states that they have been in the field upwards of sixteen months, and for the last five in a state approaching starvation from that famine which rages in that part of India, horses and cattle dying from want. Villages are deserted, and their inhabitants perishing in the camp for want of rice, which sells at a rupee per seer.

(22 Dec.)

The Commander in Chief has issued orders, that 'bat' horses shall not for the future be appropriated to any other purposes but for those for which they are intended.

By letters from Cadiz, dated the 9 Oct. we are informed, that the pestilential disease had found its way into that city, and daily carried off about 60 persons. We also learn that the disorder has extended up the Mediterranean as far as Alicante and Valencia. From Carthagena the accounts are most calamitous, as the number of deaths there is averaged at least 100 daily.

The symptoms of this terrible disorder, which is now universally allowed to be highly contagious, are the following; the patient, without any previous warning, is generally attacked with a slight giddiness, immediately followed by a severe headache, with acute pains darting inwards to the orbits of the eyes. They become red, watery and inflamed, and seem almost starting from their sockets; the pulse is hard and quick, commonly 130 in a minute; great debility almost immediately takes place which is followed by pain in the loins, and frequently violent cramps in the legs, with oppression at the breast and stupor. All these symptoms rapidly increase and generally prove fatal on the third or fourth day, and sometimes in twelve hours if not checked by proper treatment. Bleeding, which from the strong apparent determination of the disease to the head, the faculty at first frequently had recourse to, generally proved fatal, as where it subdued the fever, the patient often expired suddenly, even when thought to be out of danger. The most successful mode of treatment seems to be, first, a strong dose of glue and calomel combined with an equal quantity of jalop or rhubarb the instant the patient is attacked, to which the fever generally yields in a few hours, and afterwards to administer calomel in smaller quantities with antimonials. One surgeon who has had the prudence and firmness to pursue this plan from the beginning, has not lost a single patient.

Letters received from the Fleet of Lord Nelson to the 4 Dec. state that at that time the gallant Admiral blockaded the port of Toulon. (end of Jan.)

On the 10 inst. (Feb.) Sir Edward Pellew being then in Batancos Bay, received an overland express through Spain from Lord Nelson, who took this direct mode of informing the Government, that he was in chase of the Toulon squadron, which, with several transports, had made their escape from the port, and had been seen by neutral vessels, starting from Naples. Should his

Lordship come up with them, there will be another glorious day for England, and if they stay at Naples to land troops, they will be as open to him there as out at sea.

24, March. Letter from Lord Nelson, dated 10, Feb. Toulon. "I consider myself on the eve of a battle with the enemy's fleet, which, from the highly appointed state of the squadron under my command, will I trust, prove glorious to England." *(All this was very premature — the siege of Toulon lasted for twenty-two months.)*

Home News

Property Tax   Stow Hundred.

Notice is hereby given that the Commissioners appointed to carry into execution the general purposes of the Property Act, within the Hundred aforesaid, intend to meet on Friday, 20, July, at ten in the forenoon at the White Hart Inn, Stowmarket, when and where, all persons who have not already claimed any deductions or abatements either in respect of children, or by reason of their income being less than 150£ per annum are required to attend.

A Return under the Income Act.
I A.B. do declare
I have but little money to spare
I have
1 little maid
2 little boys
2 little trade
2 little land
2 little money at command
Rather 2 little is my little all
To supply with comfort my little squall
And 2 little to pay taxes at all.
By this you see
I have children three
Dependent on me.

The order of the day for the third reading of the Slave Trade Abolition Bill being read, Mr. Addington said, that he had been uniformly friendly to the principle of the Bill. He should support a motion in Committee to enquire into the best means of abolishing the trade; but he was conscientiously convinced that this Bill would frustrate their professed objects; that it would induce other countries to take up the trade, render the situation of the Negroes in Africa much worse than it had been, and shake the foundation of West Indian property. For these and other reasons he must vote against it.

For the Third Reading 69 — Against it 33.

The Bill was then read a third time and passed.

Act (5, Apr. 1804) for the Repeal of Duties on Windows, Houses, Servants, Carriages, Horses, Dogs, Horse-Dealers, Hair powder and Armorial Bearings.

Mr. Bolton, the ingenious and respectable artist of Birmingham has engaged to re-stamp several millions of dollars in the manner of the English silver currency, and in imitation of our crown pieces, with the difference only that the present edge-milling of the dollars is to remain. The experiment has already been successfully tried and a specimen presented to His Majesty received royal approbation.

Dollars issued at 4/9d each and those now in circulation will be received at the Bank at the present price of 5/-.

The present scarcity of silver coin will in great measure be removed.

A mechanic in Piccadilly has lately received a premium from the Society for the Encouragement of Arts and Manufactures, for the invention of a machine without a flail to thresh corn. The machine is worked by a single horse, and principally consists of a cylinder of a large magnitude, that turns horizontally and is perforated with holes, with two horizontal wheels working in unison. The grain is no ways bruised by the process.

Mrs. Mary Gurney (widow) has taken over the running of Peele's Coffee House and Tavern and Hotel at 178 Fleet-street. She continues to take in all London, Irish, Scotch and Provincial Newspapers, the old files of which go back to 1752 — the London Gazette to 1760.

A very dangerous combination has lately taken place between
the Journeymen Boot and Shoemakers, by which the masters
and the trade in general are put to the greatest inconvenience,
many industrious men being prevented from supporting their
families.

The number of Persons relieved permanently (including Child-
ren) in Workhouses in England and Wales, from returns received,
and estimated deficiency from those not received   80,492
Number of Persons relieved out of Workhouses   329,729
Number of Persons relieved occasionally   299,823
Number of Children in the Schools of Industry   20,703

By a recent inquiry into the state of mendicity in and around
the metropolis, it appears that the number of beggars, including
their children, exceeds 15,000, and that they collect from the
public in the streets about 100,000£ annually.

There is now in the Barracks at Woodbridge occupied by the
Royal Lancs. Militia, a cat which has brought up two young
chickens. Some days ago, a hen was observed sitting upon two
eggs and was frequently visited by one of the soldiers, till the
hen was missing, supposed to be killed by a dog; he immediately
took the eggs, and laid them under a cat and three small kittens,
and to the surprise and admiration of a number of people, four
days after, two chicks made their appearance, one of which
has five claws on each foot, the other only four; the whole have
lived together in the greatest harmony for this fortnight past;
when the chickens go from the cat, she immediately fetches
them back in her mouth, and is as fond of them as she is of the
kittens.

The water of the Chalybeate Spring at Wick is conceived to be as excellent a bracer as Port Wine, and is retailed at Brighton, at 6d a glass.

About 3 o'clock in the afternoon, there was a violent storm at Raydon. A fire-ball fell on a barn, while servants were stacking some wheat near it. The men saw the ball go through the thatch, and having a long ladder by them, one of the men ran up to the hole the ball had made, which appeared to him no larger than a rat-hole. He called out to his master, a ball of fire had passed through the thatch and it was on fire. The ball fell on the threshing floor about three or four feet from Mr. Wood-gate. The explosion was very tremendous, and covered a space about the circumference of a bushel, with a yellowness, similar to brimstone. He had eight acres of Dutch clover seed in and near the barn, which was all consumed, the barn totally, one door excepted; a cow-house adjoining the barn, a new erected hog-stye at some little distance with a row of new paling near the dwelling house. The farm house being near the barn, it was with some difficulty saved from the devouring flames. The farm, we hear, belongs to Dr. Neale, but unfortunately for him, the building was not insured. Mr. Woodgate was more fortunate, his furniture etc and the corn were insured in the Phoenix Fire-Office. His Hadleigh friends brought the Phoenix fire engine with them and though too late to save the barn and the cow-house, yet of great service to prevent his cornstacks from taking fire.

Nearly three millions of oranges were imported during the last week, chiefly from the Azores, there were also 340,000 oranges and lemons from Malta; the best repacked St. Michael's oranges sell at from 2£ − 2£.15s. per box. Repacked Lisbon oranges are as high as 5£ per chest.

A person at Petersbugh is in possession of a manuscript in the Russian language, written as early as A.D. 1066. It is adorned with some beautiful miniatures executed by Grecian artists. The proprietor has refused 20,000 roubles for this valuable relic; and it will be a curious fact, if, from such a source of information, it should be discovered that Russia, the history of which seems to have been involved in impenetrable darkness, should, at the period adverted to, have been the most accomplished and enlightened nation in Europe.

Among those endeavours which do honour to the piety and virtue of the age are the exertions of the Society for the Suppression of Vice. That Institution consists of more than 820 of the most respectable persons in this country. It has subsisted only since the month of June, 1802. Irregularities, denoting an open contempt of the Sabbath, were the first acts of public profligacy which it endeavoured to suppress. Reluctantly obliged to institute prosecutions against the offenders upon the laws which those irregularities violated, the Society prosecuted no fewer than 623 convictions for offences of this nature from the month of Sept. 1803 to Jan. 1804: discharged a great number upon promises to reform from such offences in future; and made between two and three thousand persons to be served with a printed warning against the offence. Finding that "not only etching, engraving, and drawing, but sculpture and modelling, especially the latter, were abused to the odious purpose of corrupting the minds of youth," that there were no fewer than 8,000 itinerant sellers of obscene prints, who travelled through the country, to retail the productions of people who thus prostituted the arts in London; the Society prosecuted seven of the most notorious and shameless of these offenders to conviction before the proper Courts.

Agricultural report for May, 1804.
A month of finer weather has rarely been experienced, and the consequence has been the utmost luxuriancy of vegetation.

Francis Sheppard, Esq. of Kitbury, near Bath entertained the Rector and nine of the parishioners to dinner. Joint ages of those present amounted to 794 years. There was not an invalid among them; they did eat heartily and drank freely and called their Host 'boy';he being but 69 years of age.

Lads under 18 years of age, if well limbed and likely to grow, may be taken, for infantry of the line or general service, as low in stature as 5'3".

The Bank has issued new dollars in exchange for those in circulation. We are very sorry, however, to find that by far the greatest number of the old dollars offered were refused, the clerks objecting to them as having counterfeit stamps. A coinage of half guineas has been delivered from the Mint to the Tower.

Well secured bond for 1785£ with interest to be Sold by Auction. To be paid on 22, Feb. 1807, with interest half yearly, by Col. Bullock, M.P. for Essex and four others of very high respectability in the said County, therefore it must be considered as good as any personal security. Auction to take place at the Baptist Coffee House in Chancery Lane.

A young widow summoned the Directresses of a Female Club, for having refused to pay her an annuity of 20£ a year, upon pretence that she had violated the rules of the society. It consists of married women of character, who pay 8/- a quarter, for which on the death of their husbands, they receive an annuity of 20£ as long as they continue virtuous widowhood. The plea of refusal was that the complainant was in the habit of being visited by a young man who frequently stayed all night in her apartment. This she admitted, but declared that the youth always sat up the whole of the night, and never attempted to take any liberties with her. Appearances, however, being against the truth of this declaration, the decision of the Magistrates was decidedly against her claim on the Club.

LOST — Went away from the Parish of Wiston near Nayland on Tuesday night or early Wednesday morning. A middle aged Woman; has been in a melancholy way for some time; had on a blue sprig gown, or a green plaid, light coloured shawl, a straw coloured calimancoe petticoat, black silk bonnet and a large bundle of things. About 5'2" rather stout and light complexion. Whoever happens on the above person and will send word so that she may be brought home will receive a due reward.

A great number of counterfeit 7/- pieces are now circulating in this town; they are extremely well finished and are not to be distinguished from the good but by weighing them; they are in general tendered by candlelight.

We hear from good authority, that the London brewers, from the extreme high price of malt, have advanced porter from 45/- to 56/- per barrel.

The Jews in several parts of Germany, when travelling, paid until lately, the same duty as was charged for *pigs!* Most if not all of the German Sovereigns, have now abolished this duty, the remains of ancient fanaticism and barbarity. The free Imperial city of Frankfurt has followed the example of the neighbouring states, and ordered this personal tax on the Jews to cease. They are, however, not yet permitted to reside but in certain streets of that city, where they are shut up every night as soon as it is dark.

The principal Farmers of Norfolk have presented a very superb piece of plate, value 600 gns. to Mr. Coke of Holkham. It is described by a gentleman who has seen it as a most beautifully embossed silver vase, near three feet in height; on its top is an elegant figurine of Ceres; round the top of the vase are embossed figures of a South Down Ram and a Devon Ox, excellently done after models from life by Mr. Garrard; on the opposite sides are figures of a Norfolk Team and Plough at work, and of Cooke's Drill, the implement generally in use for drilling the crops in Norfolk; between the handles on the same level, are a wheat sheaf and a bunch of turnips. Beneath this on one side, is Mr. Coke's arms, with the motto Prudens qui Patiens; and on the opposite side the following inscription 'Presented to Thomas William Coke, Esq. of Holkham, by the Farmers of Norfolk, as a token of their esteem for the liberality of his conduct as a Landlord, and their gratitude for the benefit of his example as a Practical Farmer, and most valuable Member of Society.'

Thursday, according to the Annual Custom, upwards of 6,000 Charity Children, attended by their Patrons, Masters and Matrons went in procession to St. Paul's Church, where an excellent and appropriate sermon was preached by the Right Rev. George, Lord Bishop of Lincoln, from 11c.5v of St. Matthew, "And the Poor have the Gospel preached to them."

New rumours are circulating respecting disturbances in Ireland.

The wife of a soldier in the Guards, lately purchased a bed of a broker in Drury-lane, and in carrying it home on her head, thought she felt something hard in it; on ripping the seam, she discovered 52gns. and two half crowns.

On Wednesday night, about 8 o'clock, as a poor watchman (whose station is at the door of Messrs. Pinchbeck & Davis, in Fenchurch-street) was going on his rounds, he picked up a bag containing 1980£ in bank notes and 50£ in cash. Much to the credit of the poor old creature, who is now 70 years of age, he immediately communicated the circumstances to several inhabitants of the street, though advised not to do so by many of his fellow watchmen, and he has paid the amount into the hands of a reputable Banker, subject to the claims of any person who can describe the contents, should such a person prove to be the owner. What renders this circumstance the more singular is, that no notice has been taken of such a loss by advertisement.

At Wisbech, there has been a steam engine erected for grinding corn which possesses the power of 80 horses and has been finished at the expence of 20,000£.

Mr. Charles Sheridan, formerly Secretary at War in Ireland, and brother to Richard Sheridan, has invented an apparatus, by which the received system of optics has been in great measure overturned; by means of which, without the assistance of mirrors, the same person or any other object, is made to appear to the human eye in three different places at the same time. It has been exhibited at the Royal Institute to the great admiration and surprize of the spectators.

A Gentleman from the country, who had heard of the number of lightfingered gentry that attended Bartholomew Fair, was determined to give them notice that they had nothing to expect from him, and walked through the Fair with his pockets turned inside out. However, on his return home, he had the mortification of finding that the skirts of his coat had been cut off.

An artist near Llanelly, has invented a cast iron nave for a wheel, which is represented as being higher, more durable and less expensive than those now in use for carts and waggons; it has also the advantage of admitting a single spoke to be replaced without disturbing any other part.

The age of Ninan L'Enclos seems to return. All the admiration and passion of the young man is transferred from the Misses of seventeen to the venerable Dames of sixty seven; or rather, the beauty of the mind and genius, can charm our present race of lovers to frenzy, when that of the person has withered. A young Irishman was, last Tuesday morning, carried before the Magistrates at the Police Office in Bow Street, by Mr. Kemble and a couple of Officers, on a charge of having, for nearly two months past, made himself troublesome to Mrs. Siddons, by love letters, and daily attempts to see her, at her house in Marlborough Street. Mr. Bond and Sir William Parsons succeeded in persuading him to desist from his courtship, by pointing out to him the folly of his conduct in making advances to a married woman. He is but twenty two years of age and a student of Lincoln's Inn.

I, James Smith, of Benhall, Labourer, do hereby give notice to all persons, not to trust, nor give credit to my wife, late Frances Howes, of Saxmundham, widow (and whose maiden name was Clack) she having voluntarily separated herself from me on Saturday last; so that I will not pay any debts she may contract on my account.

A collection was lately made at the Independent Chapel in Huddersfield for the benefit of missions to Africa, which amounted to upwards of 70£. A labouring man, who has a wife and several children depending on him for support, added to the collection, twenty guineas, being his whole saving from labour for a number of years.

A Board of General Officers declared it to be expedient that instead of the present allowance of Coals and Candles to Officers, a sum of money should be allowed for those articles; that the pay of an Ensign should be advanced to 7/- per day; that of a Lieutenant to 9/-; that of a Captain to 12s. and that Field Officers should also receive a proportional advance.

The Duke of Sussex has brought with him two High German Servants; one of them has whiskers, and his beard as long as a Jew Rabbi, and they are both powdered, and kept in particular order. The other has very long whiskers, and his beard is so long on his upper lip, that it is plaited.

General Post Office, 22 June, 1804.
His Majesty's Post Master General feels it necessary to apprize the Public, that several Actions have been brought against very respectable merchants residing in the Metropolis and at Bristol, Liverpool, Birmingham, Norwich and Ipswich for sending letters otherwise than by the post, contrary to the provisions of an Act of Parliament. The Court of the King's Bench has given leave to the parties to compound these actions, with the concurrence of the Post Master General, upon payment of one penalty and costs.

The inducement to this lenity has principally been, the short period since the passing of the Act, and the probability that the parties might err inadvertently; but their Lordships must now signify that as the Act has been in force two years, they will in future deem it incumbent on them to put the law into full effect.

The first Greek Grammar printed at Milan, 1476, with the letter of Demetrius Cretensis prefixed to it, has been found in a tower at Holkham. Likewise a manuscript of the Iliad of Homer, the same as Mr. Townley's, but better preserved, the leaves of which are one foot long and about four inches wide, consisting of 288 pages. There is also another Iliad in manuscript containing 13 books only, and an illuminated Livy, but none of the lost parts of the Roman historian. Besides these there are many treasures yet unexplored, which were brought from abroad by Lord Leicester in James I's reign.

The Eurus, store-ship, armed en flute, has been obliged to leave her station in Bantry Bay, and has returned to Plymouth, in order to get rid of the numerous rats by which she is infested.

The whole of the Hull Greenland Whalers, to the amount of no less than 40 sail, have reached port in safety. They have had one of the most successful seasons ever experienced. Not a single ship returned without a tolerable cargo. Several of them had on board 19 fish, and 337 was the amount of the fish brought by the fleet.

A few days ago, two French prisoners escaped from Norman Cross, and having cleared the vicinity of the Barracks, they took different routes; when one of them, having quitted the public road, soon met with a singular obstruction. On crossing a stile, he was attended by a shepherd's dog, of the true English breed, which obstinantly opposed his progress and repeatedly fastened on his legs and heels, till the noise attracted the attention of some passengers, and the Frenchman was ultimately reinstated in prison.

At the Bath Agricultural Meeting, the first adjudication of the annual gold medal, left by the late Duke of Bedford, and called the Bedford Medal, was made to Mr. Arthur Young, for his Essay on the Nature and Properties of Manures.

At Salisbury Michaelmas Fair the average price of good potatoes was 6s 6d a sack. Onions are in great plenty and remarkably cheap.

The Inspectors of the Hundred of Plomesgate have received instruction from the Lieutenants of the Division, to direct that the supervisors of Parishes would inspect all waggons in their Parishes and make return of such as they consider capable and fit for conveyance of Troops for which purpose it is intended to have benches slung in each waggon.

By a clause in the London Dock Warehouse Act, lately passed, it appears that no other days than Sundays, Christmas-days, Good Fridays and Fast days, are to be observed at the Docks or Warehouses as holidays. We trust that this excellent example will be generally adopted in our Public Offices.

The Master Shoemakers had no sooner brought their Journeymen to obedience, on Saturday last, than the female shoe-banders mutinied and struck for 'more wages and less work' so that, according to the report of Hobey, head of the craft, there is too much reason to expect that in future, when the shoemaking sons of St. Crispin rise, they will have an insurrection of their ladies to Boot!

East Suffolk Regiment of Militia.
JAMES SALMON, Labourer, resident of Kersey, 22 years of age, 5'5", light complexion, thin visage, grey eyes and light brown hair. Substitute for James Copeman of Beccles. Left the regiment 27, Aug. The usual reward will be paid to whoever shall apprehend the above deserter.

A very hot press had lately taken place throughout the kingdom. Even the different signal houses along the coast have been deprived of their hands, many of which are now worked wholly by landmen, under the command of a Lieutenant of the Navy.

Every window, exceeding on the outside, including the frame, 12 feet in height, or in breadth 4'9", not made prior to 5 April, 1785, nor belonging to any shop or public-house, must be reckoned and paid for as two windows.

The Magistrates hereby admonish all whom it may concern, to attend carefully to the state of the Weights and Measures used by them respectively, especially the sellers of Bread, Meat, Beer and Wine.

Tuesday the Lord Mayor ordered the price of Bread to be reduced 3d on the peck loaf; the price of the quartern loaf of wheaten is now 11½d; and the household 9¾d.

A considerable degree of curiosity has been excited at Bridlington, Yorkshire, by a little boy, who was sold by a beggar woman to a Chimney-sweeper. From the appearance, manners and language of the child, there is every reason to suppose he has been stolen. He is about four years of age, his dialect is that of the south of England and he talks of his 'papa and mamma', but cannot tell where they live. He has beautiful black eyes and eyelashes, with an high nose, and is a most interesting character. Every endeavour is making to discover his real parents.

The disorderly spirit which has so long prevailed among the Journeymen Bootmakers at the West end of the town has again manifested itself, in continued riot for the last three days. On Sunday morning, some fresh difficulties having arisen among them, a large number of Makers and Closers assembled in Oxford-road, where a general conflict ensued, and some of them were severely cut and maimed.

With a view to stop the progress of the Enemy, should they effect a landing, some works have been undertaken on the River Lea. The effect of them was tried on Monday last. The works consist of a vessel, which forms a floating gate, and fits a groove made across the bottom of the river, at the Four Mills, Bromley. This vessel being brought into the proper situation is filled with water, by means of a valve in her bottom, by which she sinks her keel, stem and stern filling the groove which has been formed for that purpose. This is done at high water, and when the tide ebbs, the vessel forms a dam and pens the water for several miles upwards. Along the different bridges on the Essex road, at Stratford and Westham, are five sluices so contrived as to confine the water as high as the lowest part of the turn-pike-road. Near to Temple Mills, are two other sluices, which confine the water to the Fishing-house, and there are two more, which enclose it to Lea-bridge and at Lea Bridge Mills the sluices have been found to pen the water to near Tottenham Mills, below which the line of defence strikes off towards Highbury.

The tide suiting at about half past one, the vessel, which is about 64' long was brought into position, the valves were opened, and in about ten minutes she sunk into her place. All the sluices were shut at the same time . . . the river was completely full in every place, and the water ready to overflow the marshes.

For nearly three weeks, the only daughter of Mr. Wright of Duke Street, Manchester Square, aged three years, appeared unwell, as if from a cold in the head and nose, she could hardly speak; and the parents, from her nose getting quite flat, began to fear it was broken by a fall. A surgeon was consulted, whose opinion was the nose was not broken, but probably the child had had a fall or a blow, as her forehead appeared black. An abscess in the left forehead seemed to be gathering. Thursday another surgeon called to see the child, and probed the nose, when he drew out a white kidney bean, swelled seven times as big as its common size when dry, and which had begun to grow in the child's head, striking upwards, and was extracted perfect, except splitting in half. The father has got it in spirits; since which the child is as well as it was before; it had somehow or other, pushed this bean up its nose, and could not get it back again.

Saturday se'nnight, about dusk, a large armed French vessel hove insight off the town of Brighton and captured two brigs and a lugger in the Road. One of the battery guns being fired, and signals of an enemy made by the telegraph, one of His Majesty's cruisers soon appeared, and retook two of the captured vessels. The Frenchman escaped with the other prize into Dieppe.

Winchester Michaelmas Fair.
Shew of Sheep not so great and ground soon cleared at very high prices. Bacon was also very dear.

The noble mansion and fine estate of Fisherwick-park, in the County of Stafford, the residence of Lord Spencer Chichester, was sold on Thursday at Garraway's Coffee House, for the sum of 143,000£, to a potatoe merchant.

Died at Stratford Parsonage the Rev. Narcissus Charles Proby.

Fifty Pounds Reward.
Information having been given that several meetings of Journeymen Fellmongers have lately been held at Public Houses and other places for the purpose of obtaining an advance of their wages, contrary to the Act of Parliament for preventing the unlawful combination of workmen, a reward of 50£ will be paid to any person or persons, who may have attended any such meeting and who will give such testimony and evidence on behalf of His Majesty, or the information now preparing, as may lead to a conviction of one or more of the principal offenders; such discovery to be made to Mr. Drew, of Bermondsey-street, the solicitor for the prosecutors, and by whom the above reward will be paid on any such conviction; and the person or persons who shall give such testimony will also (by virtue of such Act) be indemnified and discharged from any information against him or them, for any offence committed contrary thereto.

Saturday morning, five broad wheel waggons arrived at the Bank, with the specie and bullion loaded from the Spanish frigates detained at Portsmouth.

Johnson the smuggler, whose exploits on various occasions, have made so much noise in this and other countries, after having nobly resisted the temptation and menaces of the French Government to induce him to serve the enemies of Old England, has, by another piece of singular address and intrepidity, escaped from the dungeons of Bonaparte, and is now in London. It is universally admitted, that in various occupations, and in that of smuggling particularly, Johnson has acquired a more accurate knowledge of the different ports and bearings of the coasts of Great Britain, France and Holland than most others. He has obtained His Majesty's pardon, with some situation under Government. His intrepidity, activity and enterprize, certainly entitle him to repute, and his unshaken patriotism has some claim to reward.

At 7 o'clock in the morning of 18, Nov. there will be a beautiful conjunction between the planets Venus and Saturn.

Government has determined to erect a new Mint, on a scale of extent and magnificence worthy of the nation. The plan adopted, after much consideration, we understand to be, that a new edifice shall be erected on the site of the present Tobacco Warehouses on Tower Hill which occupy an area of 6 acres. Orders are said to have been issued for the coinage of a million sterling of silver currency, namely crown, half crown, shillings and sixpences.

Thursday se'nnight a contention took place in Southampton between the bakers, who through the medium of the public crier, sold bread to the poor at 17d,16d, and 15d per gallon at which price it continued to be somewhat permanently sold.

Red mullets are sold at 8d per doz.

Bacon by the half flitch at 6d per lb. and a single lb. 6½d. poultry has been abundant and at easy prices; new butter 12d per lb.

The astronomer De La Lande, has calculated that more rain has fallen within these last nine months than the 27 preceeding; to this he ascribes the fevers which afflict several counties. To console us however, he promises a very healthy, dry, but, at the same time, a very cold winter.

Notwithstanding the quantity of coals brought to London this year, exceeds that of the first ten months of last; yet, though the weather is mild and open, this necessary article sells at the exorbitant price of 70s. per chaldron, delivered to housekeepers.

Monday arrived at Torbay, the Ville de Paris, San Joseph, Prince George, Temeraire, Prince, Glory and Plantagenet, from off Brest. It has been said, that the Fleet has quitted its station, not on account of bad weather, but in consequence of a determination on the part of His Majesty's Ministers to discontinue the blockade during the winter. It is said that this determination has been adopted from a conviction that we cannot, during the winter, blockade the Port so effectually as to prevent the enemy from putting to sea. That being the case, it has been deemed improper to expose our ships to the fury of the winter storms.

The fall of snow has been so great in most of the Northern counties, that the mail coaches were detained in many parts till passages had been cut for them through the snow. (22, Dec).

Died at Chesterfield in Derbyshire aged 73 years of age, Mr. William Manley, formerly an attorney of great practice in that place. The mutability of human affairs was strongly exemplified in the fate of the deceased. His practice for several years as a solicitor was extensive, lucrative and honourable; and he was esteemed, visited and employed by many of the first families in the neighbourhood; but he departed this life in the Parish Workhouse!

He was very handsomely interred by the subscription of some liberal minded gentlemen who had formerly known him in the days of his prosperity.

2190 children have already been inoculated with the Cow Pox in the Public Dispensary at Edinburgh, and in no instance has it failed of the desired effect.

TAKEN UP — In the streets of Ipswich upon the 9th inst. A Sow and Seven Pigs. The owner of them may have them again by applying to William Brame, Inspector of the encroachment on the pavement. If they be not claimed within 14 days they will be sold for the payment of charges.

Handy hints for the Home

Lord Romney has found that parsnips are very valuable as food for cows. They are very fond of them, and yield more milk than when fed with oil-cake, or any other food.

The following is recommended as a cheap and lasting paint for gates, rails and palisades; Skimmed milk, 2 quarts; fresh slaked lime, 8 oz. boiled linseed oil, 6 oz. white Burgundy pitch, 2 oz. Spanish white, 3 lbs. Slake the lime by dipping it in water, and then expose it in the air till it falls into powder, then mix it with a fourth part of the milk, adding the oil a little at a time; stir well with a wooden spatula, adding the remainder of the milk; lastly add the Spanish white. The pitch must be previously dissolved in the oil by a gentle heat; when used, to be laid on (two coats) with a painter's brush; the expence about a half-penny a square yard.

Meat suspended in a flannel bag, will continue sweet much longer than by any of the modes generally practised. The cooler and drier the meat is when the flannel is put round it, the better. A flannel bag, with a wooden platter or bowl, is the best way to carry or keep butter.

The Potatoe is very rarely cooked in the manner it merits, and whereby it may be made into food at least as nutritious as is any species of our diet. The following is a Lancashire receipt. Sort out your potatoes as to size, scrape off the rind, put them into an iron pot (if cast iron the better) simmer them until they begin to crack, and a fork will pierce them easily; after this, pour off all the water, put away the lid of the iron pot, sprinkle over them some salt, and shake up well; after this, place the pot at the edge of the fire, and there let it remain for an hour or more; in this time, all the moisture of the potatoes will gradually exhale steam, and you will find them (be the sort of growth what it may) white and flakey as snow, and in such a state of eating, as those only can judge who have tried them. Take out with a spoon or a ladle.

Tea kettles, furred with stoney concretions, may be cleaned by occasionally boiling potatoes in them; potatoes being boiled in a new kettle, no concretations will afterwards form.

To detect the deleterious effects of adulterated malt-liquor, dip a heated tobacco-pipe into the liquor, and if any noxious ingredients be infused therein, it will return black; but on the contrary, a pure white.

An excellent cement has been prepared lately by the French Chemists, from common cheese. The method is this; cut the cheese in pieces, and boil it in water, stirring it with a spoon until it be reduced to a glutinous state. Then throw off the remaining water not evaporated, and pour cold water upon the substance. Let it then be pressed or kneaded, and renew the change of water several times. Pound the mass afterwards upon a stone or in a mortar. In two days the cement will be fit for use, will be wholly insoluble in water, and may be employed on wood, marble etc, and the union of the fractured parts will be so perfect as to render it very difficult to discover the intersection.

Friction with common oil is an excellent remedy for the yellow fever, united with other means hitherto employed. Gen. Reden, commander of the Swiss regiment, employed it on himself and soldiers, and did not lose a single man of the 1600 of whom his corps consisted.

Marriages and Deaths

EPIGRAM
Tis true my Friend, that Lydia's voice
Engag'd my ravish'd ear.
My heart almost made her my choice
My future hours to cheer.
But absent, quite secure I stood
Nor wish'd to take the pill
For Lydia's notes, however good,
Won't pay the Butcher's bill.

Last week was married in Cambridgeshire, Mr. James Gordon, a Serjeant in His Majesty's forces, to Miss Nancy Pitcher, with a fortune of 5000£. Miss Pitcher was in the constant habit of attending the evening parade, where the fine figure and manly appearance of the Serjeant made a deep impression on her heart. She was not long in disclosing her passion for him; for one evening a friend of her's called the Serjeant from parade, and acquainted him with her attachment. The gallant Son of Mars immediately closed with the proposal.

The nuptials of Lady Sarah Fane and Lord Villiers were celebrated on Wednesday night. The happy couple dined together at the home of the earl of Westmoreland. At ten o'clock the marriage ceremony was performed in the grand Saloon by Dr. Bennet, the Bishop of Cloyne. Lord Westmoreland and Lady Sarah's two sisters were present. The bride was most elegantly attired in a Brussels lace robe, with Brussels lace cloak and veil, which cost upwards of 500 gns.

In the list of recent marriages is that of Mr. Cook to Miss Mutton, both of Market Harborough, by the Rev. Mr. Gravey. This marriage seems to promise a dish of house lamb next season.

Last week in Lincolnshire, Chevalier D'aragon, formerly of the Parliament of Normandy to Miss Barbara Mitchell with a fortune of 20,000£.

A shoemaker, residing on Saffron-hill, who had the misfortune of being married to a woman who used frequently to beat him, on Thursday obtained a warrant against her for an assault. An American sailor, a mutual friend known in the neighbourhood by the name Old Tom, after ineffectually labouring to reconcile the parties, at length proposed to buy the termagant. The proposal was eagerly acceded to; he paid down half a guinea, and the expence of the warrant, and the lady was transferred to him.

On the 14th.inst. was married at Gretna Green, R.H. Vivian, Esq. Major of the 7th Light Dragoons, to Miss Eliza Champion Crespigny.

On Monday, 22nd October, was married at Malton, Mr. R. Wood, of the Blue Boar Public House of that place, to Mrs. Sarah Murrill, late Housekeeper to John Webb Weston, Esq. of Guildford. This marriage took place in consequence of an advertisement for 'A Wife' which appeared in the York Herald in July last. The advertisement being read by the Lady's maid, she immediately showed it to the Housekeeper, telling her it would be a good match for her. After some little correspondence, an interview took place at Grantham, and the lady was brought down to Malton, to see the situation. Everything proving agreeable, the marriage was speedily consummated.

An odd wedding was celebrated last week at a village in Berkshire. The bridegroom was 88 years of age, the bride 83, the father 91, and the two ladies who officiated as bride-maids

above 70; neither of the latter had been married. Six grand
daughters of the bridegroom strewed flowers before the
company on their way to and from the Church.

(Note: There appears to be a discrepancy here in the ages of some of those concerned!)

A gentleman in Lincolnshire lately married his Housekeeper,
that he might leave her his property. In four days after, she
attended him to the grave. Friday se'nnight, she was married
to a cobbler with seven children.

At a wedding lately in a country church in Somersetshire, we
are told, the bride, who had been by her worthy Pastor well
grounded in the Church Catechism, and who had not, perhaps
studied the matrimonial service with the laudable zeal, which
many ladies think necessary, upon being asked, as usual, the
question, "Will thou have this man to thy wedded husband?"
cut short the Clergyman, by innocently replying, "Yes, verily;
and by God's help, so I will; and I heartily thank our Heavenly
Father that he hath called me to this state."

Lately was married at Sheffield, Mr. William Green, farmer, of
Hallam in Yorkshire aged 75 years to Miss Sarah Worrall, aged
30. The lady had been formerly an apprentice to the old gentleman, who during fifteen years of hard courtship, had many
opportunities of becoming acquainted with her worth. During
the nuptial ceremony, which was witnessed by hundreds of
people, the clergyman's voice being too feeble to convey to the
deaf bridegroom any idea of the happiness he was conferring,
the Clerk was obliged to act as a mouthpiece and shout the
blessing into poor old William's ears. We are informed that
William has been at the altar before, having given an early proof
of his discretion in chusing a wife, by marrying a woman of
75, when he was only 25.

Last Sunday as a party of young men were playing at Cricket in Wokingham, Edward Kimble, aged 23 years, who was eagerly engaged in the game, dropped down and expired immediately. Let those who devote this sacred day to similar pleasures, take heed lest they fall.

Monday, died Miss Deborah Atkins, eldest daughter of the Rev. Atkins, Dissenting Minister in this town. Although she had not completed the tenth year of her age, such was the influence of religion upon her mind, that it enabled her to bear with patience and resignation a long and painful affliction, raised her superior to the fear of death and afforded her a pleasing cheerful hope of a blessed mortality.

Sir Francis and Lady Sykes's infant family arrived last Saturday at Yarmouth from Germany, their parents arrived before them, but alas! both in their coffins. The mother caught a fever attending to the children which was communicated to the father as he watched by the bed of his wife and both fell victims almost at the same moment.

A short time ago died, Scotch Maggy, alias Mary Grey, alias Wheeler, alias Barnsley — universally admitted to be the most expert pick-pocket in England. She came originally from Scotland and married one of the notorious Wheelers, with whom she lived some years. On the arrival of another notorious pick-pocket from Botany Bay, of the name of Barnsley, she took a great fancy to him and left her husband.

She generally dressed in a very genteel style. About seven years ago, she was in Bath, committing her depredations, and at one of the Churches received the Sacrament; at the same time the Mayoress of Bath happened to be one of the Communicants; Maggy, observing her to have a very valuable gold watch, contrived to rob her of it, before the conclusion of the solemn ordinance.

She had several children, whom she kept at Boarding School. Notwithstanding she had been several times tried for capital charges, she was always fortunate enough to escape punishment.

Thursday died at Huntingdon, near Hereford, Mr. Sam Tully, an eminent farmer and breeder of cattle, of that place, and brother to Mr. Tully of Bath. The death of this truly worthy man was occasioned by a violent attack made upon him the preceding Tuesday by a favourite bull belonging to his own stock, which turned upon him and forced him to the ground with such violence with his head, as to break several of his ribs, and occasioned so much other injury, that he survived the accident only two days. Mr. Tully stood pre-eminent as a breeder of cattle; and his stock, which has so long attracted the admiration of the amateurs, has successfully gained the first prize at the Smithfield Shew, for a number of years.

Died at Holkham-hall, in the seventieth year of his age, J. Hawkesworth, many years gamekeeper to T.W. Coke, Esq. He was an eccentric character; as he rarely associated with, or spoke to any person, unless he was first addressed. He was very penurious, had accumulated a considerable fortune, which he had hid from fear of invasion; and his death was supposed to be occasioned by depriving himself of sufficient nourishment. Mr. Coke always furnished him with proper liveries; but his dress was of the most miserable kind and he always wore an old painted hat patched over with pieces of cloth. The liveries he had by him at the time of his death and which he had never worn, are supposed to be worth 100£. He was known amongst his neighbours by the title of the Walking Obelisk.

Carter, the composer, who lately paid the debt of nature, did not always meet with all the encouragement to which his musical talents might have entitled him, and as economy was not amongst the virtues which he cultivated most, he was

often reduced to those straits and difficulties from which genius
and talents can plead no exemption. In one of those scenes of
embarrassment his means and resources having been exhausted,
he ransacked the various pieces of composition he had by him,
but finding that none nor all of them could produce a single
guinea at the music shops, he hit upon the following expedient
for the immediate supply of his most pressing necessities.
Being well acquainted with the character of Handel's manuscript, be procured an old skin of parchment, which he prepared
for the purpose to which he meant to turn it, and imitating as
closely as he could the handwriting, as well as the style and
manner of the great master, he produced in a short time a piece,
which so well deceived a music seller, that he did not hesitate
to give 20 gns. for it, and the piece passes amongst many for
the genuine production of Handel to this day.

Situations Vacant and Wanted

TO NOBLEMEN AND GENTLEMEN

Wants a Situation as Agent or Steward, A very respectable Man, who has been regularly bred up to husbandry, and has a general knowledge of Farming Business, buying, etc, selling stock, and understands accompts well, the value of lands, timber, etc. and is well acquainted with the various soils in many different counties, with the different manner and ways of cultivation, particularly that of Suffolk and Norfolk.

The most respectable references will be given, and security, if required. Should this meet the eye of any nobleman or Gentleman who may have a vacancy of this kind, may depend on the advertiser his utmost assiduity and attention, to do justice to his employer, and to acquit himself with credit and respect.

A line addressed to B.W. Peele's Coffee-house, Fleet-street, will meet with due attention.

Wants a situation as Teacher in Private Family, a steady Person, who has been used to that capacity, and who is capable of assisting in household affairs. Letters addressed to E.B. and left at Mr. Rackham's, printer, Bury St. Edmunds, will be attended to.

Wants a Situation as Upper Servant in a small regular Family, a person who has lived several years in genteel families, and perfectly understands pastry, pickling etc. and would have no objection to superintend the cooking; can give the most satisfactory reference to her last situation.

Wants a Situation, A Young person who perfectly understands the Mantua and Corset making; wishes to engage herself as a lady's maid.

To Sporting Noblemen and Gentlemen
Simon Nunn, who has lived in the Capacity of Gamekeeper for
seven years in one, and nine years in another family of distinction and who has had the honour of breaking dogs to the
perfect satisfaction of the Duke of Marlborough, the Marquis
of Townsend, the Earl of Clermont, with a long list of etcs.,
purposes to be at Ipswich on the 10th. September and takes
the opportunity of offering his services to the Noblesse and
Gentry of the County of Suffolk, in the capacity of DOG
TEACHER. Letters or messages, left at Mr. Goulding's
perfumer, Carr Street, will be most punctually attended to.

Simon Nunn looks for neither pecuniary reward nor
character, unless dogs, when returned, meet the approbation of
his employers.

SHIPMEADOW HOUSE of INDUSTRY
A Special Meeting of the Directors and Acting Guardians of
the Poor, in the Hundred of Wangford, is ordered to be held at
the above House, for the purpose of electing a Governor and
Matron to take upon them the care and management of the
Poor in the said House from Michaelmas next.

The Governor must understand the business of wool and
tow spinning, and have a knowledge of the farming business.

Wanted immediately, A Person not under 18 years of age, of
good disposition, who writes well and understands general rules
of Arithmetic, as an Assistant in a Boarding School in Essex.

Wanted: Two Apprentices of Genteel connection to the
Millinery and Fancy Dress making, who will have the opportunity of being instructed in all the changes of fashion every
month. Personal applications or letter, post paid, addressed to
Mrs. Symond, Wangford, will be duly attended to. A premium
will be expected.

Wanted as WET NURSE, the beginning of November, A respectable married Woman, of a very healthy constitution, who can have an undeniable character of sobriety, honesty, cleanliness and good temper.

None need offer themselves who do not fully answer the above description; as it is for a Gentleman's family the person is wanted, and where wages (should the person suit) are no particular object.

Apply in person or by letter to Mr. Edwards, Surgeon, Long Melford.

Wanted as Dairy Maid in a Gentleman's Family, a steady active Woman, not under 35 years of age, who understands the dairy business in all its branches; she will have the care of 4 cows, and will superintend a boy who feeds the pigs; she must understand baking and the management of poultry.

No one need apply who cannot produce the most undeniable references to character.

Wanted immediately for the parish of Felixstow, A Man to serve under the New Defence Act.
Apply to the Churchwardens.

Wanted for a Gentleman's family in London a Person who understands all branches of Cooking.

Wages to be paid 11gns per annum with 1gn. for Tea.

If the person will undertake both the cooking and the dairy then her wages will be per annum 12 gns. — 16 gns.

Crime and Punishment

A crime unparalleled in this country was perpetrated on Monday evening about 8 o'clock in Hanging Wood, near Woolwich. The circumstances of which were of a nature that we scarce know how to describe. As a young man was walking in the wood for his recreation, he was laid hold of behind by two persons, who laid him flat on his face, then turned him on his back and gagged him; all this while he saw them not; one laid himself on his breast, while the other, by a surgical operation, unmanned the unfortunate youth, and afterwards closed the wound by sewing up the same with glazed silk. In this extraordinary condition he was found by those whom his cries called to his relief. In a very weak and almost senseless state he was taken to the town, when all the surgeons of the garrison attended him, and they entertain hopes of his recovery. The sufferer is a young man about 22 years of age and a labourer in the dock. There is no accounting for the circumstances, but on the supposition that the perpetrators of this vile deed mistook the object of their resentment.

A Mr. Stuckbury was last Tuesday convicted in the Court of King's Bench, of an assault, with intent to ravish a young married lady, the wife of Mr. Keltie, of Wardour-street. He came accidentally into company with her at a Coffee-house to which she attended her mother and sister, who there awaited a coach in which they were to go to the country. He offered to protect her as she walked back to her own house, led her into a court, forced her into a house of ill fame, and would there have accomplished his purpose, but for the lady's resolute virtue.

Tuesday, a coachman in a gentleman's family, top of Gray's Inn Lane, where he was only three weeks, was apprehended by several Parish Officers, charged with having married five young women, all now living. He is an extremely ordinary fellow, about forty years of age. The last wife is about 18 years of age, and he only married to her about three months.

William Lott was fined 20£ and sentenced to one year in Ipswich Gaol for attempting to abduct Sarah Ann Morgan. He attempted to force her into a chaise with intent to carry her off, in which he was assisted by James Paine.

On Sunday night, the Post Horse-office in Poland-street, was broken open by the most violent exertions. The lock of the street door, which is extremely strong, was set into the wall, but the violence used was so great, that it was forced out of the wall. The villains proceeded to break open the front office; they then broke open the clerk's desk, which only contained a 20£ note, with which they made off. On Friday was the general receiving day, the receipts of which amounted to 30,000£ and it is supposed the villains were apprised of this and expected to get possession of this sum.

Information to the amount of several hundreds are said to have been laid against the confectioners for selling Ices, etc. on the Sabbath.

An Action was brought for £40.8s.6d., the charge for food, lodging and protection for the offspring of seduction.

The Judge said, "the sustenance of natural children was not only a sacred and moral obligation, but a legal one." However, if the child is taken from the custody of the father then he is no longer liable. Action for the Plaintiff was granted.

Saturday, James Combes, alias Jethro Cheesman, was executed at Reading for horse stealing. Since his condemnation he has slept in his coffin every night; his conduct at the place of execution was resolute and determined; seemingly insensible of his awful situation; he met his fate with apparent unconcern.

William Notley was committed to Bury Gaol charged with threatening to set fire to the Workhouse at Clare.

In the Court of the King's Bench, the King v John Apple and others. This was an indictment for a nuisance. The defendants lived in Willow-court, Goswell-street and were manufacturers of Prussian blue, the process of making of which, emitted a most violent stench, and on this the complaint was grounded. The principal ingredients made use of were the horns and hoofs of animals, reduced by fire, and in that state infused, with ashes, vitriol, allum, etc. which being stirred up, sent forth a volume of thick black smoke, and being too heavy to rise and disperse, spread around and annoyed the neighbourhood by its abominable smell. It appeared upon the cross examination of the first witnesses, that besides this manufactory, there was a soap lees man, a soap boiler's, a tallow melter's, a dye-house with a steam engine, a burying ground, a night man's, a horse boiler's, a drug grinder's, a starch maker's, a skinner's distillery, two or three hog butchers, a soda manufactory, and various other equally odiferous trades, within the circumference of 200 yards, and the witness confessed, when they were all at work, he could not discriminate which smell was the worst. It appeared further, that the tallow maker's was by much the most disagreeable at times, and that an indictment had been brought against him some time ago, upon which he had been acquitted. The defendants had been carrying on the business for several years without any complaints being made against them and there appears no reason for the present particular distinction.

Defendants Not Guilty.

Francis Smith, convicted last January of having committed a capital crime, in shooting a man at Hammersmith, when he supposed he had seen a ghost, has received His Majesty's free pardon.

An Overseer of the Poor of the Parish of Lidlington (Beds.) was indicted for dismissing a woman from his service, she being, at the time of the dismissal, actually in labour, without making any provision for her relief. It came out, in evidence, that both the master and mistress of the woman (the Overseer and his wife) were well acquainted with the state in which she was; that they refused to receive her back into their house, upon her entreaty to be so received; and that the Overseer ordered one of his labourers to walk with her as far as Ampthill, a distance of three miles and upwards, and there leave her at the first public house. The Jury found a verdict of Guilty, and the Court sentenced the Overseer to an imprisonment of two months and 20£ fine.

Amongst several convictions last week at Leeds, one was that of a waggoner for following his business on a Sunday; and eight persons paid the penalty of 3s 6d. each and all expences, for bathing in a public part of the river on Sunday during the time of divine service.

A Gentleman in the County of Essex, about 70 years of age, was some time ago charged before a Magistrate by his House-keeper, who is about fifty years of age, with violently attempting to rob her of her chastity, which she fortunately preserved from the attacks of the old Gentleman. Swearing positively to these facts, the accused was held to bail in the recognisance of 400£ to appear to the charge of our next Assizes.

A Volunteer who received his guinea but did not attend when required was sentenced to receive 200 lashes, to be drummed out of the Corps and to refund the guinea. The Commanding Officer, after a suitable admonition, was pleased to remit that part of the sentence ordering corporeal punishment.

Monday last, a man, for taking away muck at an improper hour and dropping a considerable quantity of it in the streets of this town, was convicted before the Magistrates and paid the mitigated penalty of 12s.

Whereas I Samuel Bridges of Worlingworth, bricklayer, having propagated a scandalous report, tending to injure the character of Elizabeth, daughter of Mr. John Shearing, farmer, and the said Mr. Shearing being determined to prosecute me for the same, but out of lenity to my wife and family has agreed to forbear so doing on my making acknowledgement in this public manner, and paying all expences. Now I do hereby declare the said report to be entirely false and groundless, and do hereby beg pardon of the said Mr. Shearing and also of Elizabeth his daughter, and return thanks for the lenity shown to me and my family, and I do hereby promise never to offend in like manner.

Gen. Barton, of Chelsea, was recently brought before a Court Martial, for duelling with an inferior officer.

Thursday in the afternoon during the Races, two silver table spoons, a striped single breasted waistcoat and a cotton pocket handkerchief were stolen from the dwelling house of Mr. Freeman, draper and taylor.

Joseph Jackson and Thomas Bucknell, the victims of the violated laws of their country, were on Thursday morning brought from Newgate to the usual place of execution, in order to suffer the dreadful punishment annexed to the crime of forgery. It is with regret we say, that they did not meet their fate with that firmness and resignation which would have become them as men and Christians. When the inferior Officers of Justice attended to conduct them from their cell to the scaffold, they found them in a situation which too clearly indicated they had attempted to destroy themselves. They had taken poison; but it was either not of sufficient virulence, or not administered in such a way as to destroy life. It produced only a sort of lethargy, but not to that degree as to prevent the unfortunate men from feeling the wretchedness into which their guilt had plunged them. They were obliged to be supported on the platform by the executioner and his assistants, who observed, that they had never seen men quit life with less courage. The weak state to which they had reduced themselves rendered their passage to eternity but of short duration. They expired without a struggle.

Friday evening, as Mr. and Mrs. Disney of Surbiton-house were returning from town in a curricle, they were stopped near Kingstone, and robbed of two watches and 32£ in notes.

The celebrated John Benjamin Pritchard, alias Price, has escaped from the Bridewell, Norwich by forcing the staple off the wicket belonging to his cell, and putting his hand through and picking the padlock attached to the cell door. He then went upstairs, picked another lock, and fastened his sheet, which he had rent to pieces, to one of the windows; came down and picked the lock of the door that goes into the yard; drew himself by the sheeting on the roof of the prison; and let himself down on the outside in the same manner. All this he accomplished without detection. And as the utmost care had been used to prevent his receiving any instrument, it may be supposed that this was executed without any other tool than a nail.

Samuel Miles Mitchell was committed to Newgate, on his own confession, for the wilful murder of his daughter, a child of nine years of age, by deliberately taking her by the hair of her head, as she sat by the fire, and with a razor nearly severing her head from her body. When the Magistrate desired him to sign the confession, he exclaimed, "Yes, I will, with the same hand that did the bloody deed." This person must be insane.

William Brown was found guilty of stealing a hempen shirt and other wearing apparel the property of Joseph Orford and ordered to be transported for seven years.

Broke out of Bridewell, Sam Pollard, he is of a fair complexion, light brown hair, his nose somewhat turned up at the end; about 5' 9", 30 years of age, by trade a linen weaver and has formerly travelled with hempen cloth; was dressed in a dark velveret frock and breeches; the frock has been let out in the sleeves and sides, and striped waistcoat. Whoever will apprehend the said Sam Pollard and convey him to Botesdale Bridewell, or lodge him in any of His Majesty's gaols, shall receive a reward of 20£, by applying to John Bond, keeper of the said Bridewell.

A Private in the Coldsteam Guards was ordered 300 lashes at a Court Martial for pretending to be a crippled beggar in off duty hours.

Charles Browne, Apprentice to Mr. Seager, Breeches-maker of Grundisburgh, having run away from his said master and not having been heard of for the last three weeks, is hereby invited to return to his mother, Elizabeth Reynolds of Coddenham, she having purchased the remaining term of his apprenticeship.

A term of six months imprisonment was imposed on the striking hatters who refused to work with one Hurns who would not join their union. Justice Grose, with great energy commented on the evils which would arise in this commercial country if the inferiors in trade were permitted thus to conspire and to frame laws on which the occupation of their masters and men of property depended.

Thursday evening, about quarter past seven, the Right Honourable Dowager, Lady Dacre, was taking her usual solitary walk near her house at Lee between Lewisham and Eltham in Kent; when a ruffian came up, presented a pistol and demanded her watch. She told him if he would take the pistol away, she would give it him. As soon as he had the watch, he put the pistol again to her Ladyship's breast and demanded her purse. This she also gave; it contained six guineas, with which the villain immediately departed. It may be necessary to inform some of our readers, that ever since the death of the late Lord Dacre, this amiable widow has made it an invariable practice to visit his tomb at a certain hour every evening. No company, no engagement, no inclemency of weather, neither storms nor hurricanos, have ever prevented her from executing this pious office.

The Toll-gate keeper at Rushmere was convicted before the Magistrates in the full penalty of 40s. for having demanded and received payment of toll from a member of the 2nd. Corps of Suffolk Yeomanry Cavalry, when he was properly accoutred, and going to the field of exercise.

Robert Howell was brought before the sitting Magistrate James
Reid, Esq. at the Public Office, Bow-street, on a charge of
having robbed a poor, blind sailor. Francis Cooke, the blind
sailor, deposed that he was discharged from the hospital ship,
the Sussex, lying at Sheerness, on the 23rd. of last month; and
the prisoner, who was also an invalid, and who had been his
brother shipmate several years, was appointed his guide to
conduct him to Bristol. They landed somewhere in London,
where he couldn't tell; it was night, and the prisoner tore off
his jacket, in which his money was sewed up, amounting to 7£
in bank notes; took his stick from him, and two bags containing
his clothes, leaving him in the street almost naked and penny-
less; he was picked up by a watchman and passed from one
watchman to another, till he made his way to Bow-street. He
then identified the prisoner's voice, and his own clothes, which
he swore to by the feel, distinguishing plain from cheque shirts;
he identified his pantaloons by their short cut, his trowsers by
being dirty and folded in a particular manner; but most
particularly a blue spotted handkerchief by a white darn in one
corner. He was committed to take his trial at the next Sessions;
the Magistrate observed, that it was impossible he could be a
British sailor, but some miscreant who had crept unnoticed into
the Navy.

Tuesday at the Public Office, Union Hall, two persons were
convicted in 5£ each for selling Fireworks, on the 5th. November to a number of young persons; who were also convicted in
the penalty of twenty shillings each for firing off the same.

It may be gratifying to the public to learn that Francis Cook,
the blind sailor, who was robbed by his comrade, has been
restored to his perfect sight. His disease was considered by the
most able practitioner in town to be Gutta Serena, and therefore past a hope of remedy. The cure was effected by an
eminent surgeon of Wiveliscombe in Somerset, of the name of
Sully, who has performed some very extraordinary cures in
this way.

Thomas Smith, convicted at Dorchester Assizes of the murder of Ann Clerk, was found on the day fixed for his execution, dead in his cell, having by some means got off the cord which fastened his hands behind him, and fixed it to the bar of the window and round his neck, and then by a sudden plunge dislocated his neck. He was immediately taken to the new drop on the Porter's Lodge and there hung up, where he remained about seven hours, to gratify the curiosity of hundreds of spectators.

Tuesday se'nnight some person or persons entered the parish church of Wicklewood, Norfolk, by forcing the iron bar out of the chancel window, broke open the chest with a pick that stood near by it, and stole the Communion Cup, Plate and surplice. They have not yet been discovered.

At Middlesex Sessions, Thomas Hansard, a printer, residing in Turnstile, Holborn, was indicted for assaulting and criminally abusing a young girl of the name of Amelia Dixon, who seemed to be about 16 and remarkably pretty, and was servant to the prisoner. He was sentenced to three months in prison.

Tuesday, two men were sent on board the Monmouth, lying in Yarmouth Roads, by order of the Mayor of Norwich; one for cruelly treating his wife, and the other for an attempt on the innocence of a child of eight years.

A young woman of very genteel appearance, inquired of several of the inhabitants in Blackfriars-road, for a woman who had lain-in, but could not mention any name. She was at length directed to the house of one Martin, a porter in Currier's Row, whose wife was delivered of a boy about five weeks since; she introduced herself to the mother as having come from Portsmouth, was greatly fatigued, and gave her a seven shilling piece to buy some tea and sugar. After being refreshed, she requested Mrs. Martin to accompany her over Blackfriars Bridge to a Gentleman's house and proposed carrying the child for her. As they came to the London side of the bridge, the strange lady, in the crowd, decamped with the child, and has not since been heard of, although every possible search has been made after them; the mother is in the greatest distress of mind.

Whereas a stout thick set Man about 5'5" or 8" high, full face, dark complexion, rather pale, with a mark on his left cheek, supposed to be occasioned by the Small-pox, short dark hair, had on a blue coat with a black collar, light coloured waistcoat, shabby round hat, military boots and dirty white leather breeches, plated spurs, without under straps, and had an old saddle with one of the flaps almost off, did on Monday, 16th, change away A Stolen Horse with Mr. Thomas Randall of Snape for an aged Brown Bay Gelding.

Richard Mortlock, servant to Mr. Frost of Bentley, was convicted in the penalty of ten shillings on his own view, for riding on the shafts of his master's waggon with six horses; he was driving very rapidly, without any person by the side of the horses to guide them.

Sarah Dean received 4 months and one shilling fine, for stealing 18 yards of cotton. The light sentence was occasioned by the fact that the miscreant had been so long on remand.

Tuesday, a Chinaman, of the name of Arpane, being sworn at the Public Office, Shadwell, agreeable to the custom of his country, by taking a China saucer, and striking it violently against a piece of iron, by which means it broke into a thousand pieces, wishing that his body might break into as many pieces, if what he was going to say was not true. He stated, that he was enticed to a house of ill fame, where he was robbed of 17 dollars, by a woman who had absconded. The landlord of the house being concerned in the transaction, offered to compromise the business, but the Chinese held him fast until an officer arrived, who took him to the Office; where, from circumstances that appeared, he was fully committed for trial, and search is made for the woman.

Whereas on Friday Night, between the hours of 12 and 1 o'clock, a person on horse back, in military dress, did, in a most wanton and brutish manner, assault and ill use the Toll-keeper, at the Rushmere Turnpike Gate, without any cause whatever, and by horrid threats putting the said Toll-keeper in fear of his life, he was the last person that passed the Gate that night. Whoever will give such information as may be the means of bringing him to justice, shall, on his conviction, receive five guineas reward.

Essex Highway Misdemeanor.
We Mark Springhead and Robert Richer, servants of Mr. John Hunt of Colchester, brewer, having been convicted before a Magistrate of great misbehaviour, by interrupting Mr. Robert Dawson of Great Bentley, and two Ladies in a chaise on the highway in the parish of Elmstead, and refusing to turn out of the road, did thereby incur the penalty required by law, but in consideration of our asking pardon, paying all expences and promising in this advertisement, never to offend again in like manner, the penalties have been considerably mitigated.

Twenty seven insolvent debtors were discharged on Thursday at the Surrey Sessions; among whom were the noted pugilist Daniel Mendoza and Mr. Lockyer Wainwright, lately convicted of taking away a Ward in Chancery.

The Sporting Life

A grinning match lately took place near Bridlington, for a quantity of tobacco. There were three competitors for the prize, all of whom were seized with the most painful symptoms, in consequence of their violent contortions, and two of them died in a few days; the third lies dangerously ill.

We are informed that a third has now shared the same fate. The father of the latter, who went to visit him, was so shocked at his son's dreadful afflictions, that on his return home, he took to his bed and died a few days afterwards.

Mrs. Thornton, the Lady of Col. Thornton of Thornville Royal, is to ride a match at York Races against Mr. Flint for 1500 gns.

A certain dashing young man of large fortune lost, the other evening, at a subscription house at the West End of the town, 80,000£ — a sum greater than his whole property would pay. The winner is a person of high rank. The unfortunate gamester gave another proof of his enterprising genius by doubling the stakes, and by this hazardous manoeuvre he recovered his losses, and won a considerable sum of his antagonist.

On Monday a desperate battle was fought on Willesden Green, on the Edgware Road, between Thomas Blake, a sailor and Holmes, a Hackney coachman of Knightsbridge. The match was for 20 gns. After 60 rounds Blake was declared the victor, amid the shouts of the spectators. Considered by connoisseurs one of the best ever fought, the match lasted 1 hour 20 minutes.

Samuel Rudland was sentenced to 14 days solitary confinement in the House of Correction for allowing unlawful games to be played in his house, on Wednesday, 17 Oct. at 10' o'clock at night, when between 20 and 30 workmen assembled and were gambling with dice.

Ipswich Races	Tues. Wed. & Thurs. 3,4, & 5 July.
Tuesday.	His Majesty's Purse. 100 gns.
	Three year olds 7.11 lbs.
	Four year olds 9.5 lbs.
	Best of three 2 mile heats.
Wednesday.	Gentlemen's Purse. 50£
	For three year olds
	Heats about 2¼ miles.
	Winner to be sold for 200 gns. within ¼ hour after race.
	Owner of 2nd horse to be given first refusal.
Entrance	2 gns. 10s 6d. to Clerk of Course . . . Subscribers.
	3 gns. 1 gn. ” ” ” Non Subscribers.
Thursday	Town Purse 50£.

It is hoped that all persons, for their own safety, as well as for that of the riders of the race horses, will leave the course clear and retire behind the cords whilst the horses are running. A bell will be fixed up on the Stewards' Stand to warn all persons to keep clear of the course, previous to the horses starting.

On Sunday morning a very heavy butcher, residing near Honey-lane Market, weighing 16 stone, undertook for a wager to walk 10 miles on the Barnet road, in two hours; which to the astonishment of many friends, he actually performed in 1 hour 49 mins.

A curious wager was decided a short time since by a baker at Wethersfield, who undertook for a bet of one guinea, to drive his boar half a mile on the turnpike road between that place and Horseheath, and to ride him back within an hour, which he performed with great ease in thirty five minutes.

Monday evening a gentleman who had engaged to walk from
Hull to Driffield and back again, for a wager of 200 gns. to
100, set off from the end of Prospect-street, and reached
Driffield about a quarter past twelve. He returned to Hull about
4.15 a.m. eleven minutes within the limited time.

Mr. Yallop, of Norwich, who obtained a 16th of a 200£ prize,
in a former lottery, is the holder of a 16th share of No. 9219,
drawn a prize of 20,000£, and Friday se'nnight, Mr. Denny
Crabb, a farmer of Wattisfield, is the holder of a share of No.
14,002, a prize of 500£, and the person who drives the London-
Fakenham stage coach, has gained a part of a 10,000£ prize.

Shocking Accidents

On the 11 September, a seaman of the Victory, of 110 guns, Lord Nelson's flagship, fell from the forecastle into the sea; on hearing the cry of a man overboard, Mr. Edward Flin, a volunteer, jumped from the quarter deck after him and had the good fortune to save the man, notwithstanding the extreme darkness of the night and the ship at the time being under sail. The next morning Lord Nelson sent for Mr. Flin, and presented him with a Lieutenant's commission, appointing him to the Bittern sloop of war; and at the same time told him he would strongly recommend him to the Lords of the Admiralty.

Monday morning as three Caulkers were standing on a stage caulking a ship at Shadwell Dock, the rope which suspended the stage, gave way, when they were precipitated to the bottom of the dry dock; one was killed upon the spot, two were taken to the hospital; one of whom died on Tuesday, the other is not expected to recover.

A young woman was on Monday evening crossing the road with a child in her arms, near the Small-Pox Hospital, Pancras, and was thrown down by a gentleman's carriage that was driving along with great fury. The child died almost immediately, and the young woman was not expected to live many hours.

As some Gentleman were lately fishing in Walney Channel, they killed three sharks, evidently sick and exhausted. On opening them, there was found, in the belly of one of them, a pair of buckskin breeches, a man's hand and a diamond ring, marked 'B! It is conjectured that these ravenous fishes had followed some ships from the westward.

The lifeless body of Fanny White of Lambeth (17) was retrieved from the Serpentine where she drowned herself after discovering that she had been bigamously married a few days earlier. A half-penny was found in her bosom.

It is reported that Mr. Garnham Steadman, son of Mr. J. Steadman of Ixworth eloped with the beautiful daughter of Mr. Boldero, an opulent farmer of the same place. Pursued by Mr. Boldero, by the carelessness of the driver, the chaise unfortunately upset, and Mr. B. was most dreadfully bruised. He lingered but two hours before he expired.

Tuesday se'nnight, a boy employed to sweep a chimney in the house of Mr. Saville, in Devereaux-court had got to the top of the chimney when the chimney pot gave way, and fell with the ill-fated youth into the yard adjoining the house, and he was killed on the spot.

As the son of Mr. Wiseman was riding the shaft-horse in an empty harvest waggon, the animal fell down, which frightening the other two horses, they ran away with the waggon, dragging the young man and the horse till the rein he held broke, when the wheel went over his body and he received very severe injuries, but hopes are entertained of his recovery.

A young lady was observed, on Monday, about 1 o'clock, by the guard at Buckingham-gate, to throw herself into the Canal in St. James's Park. Assisted by a waterman, the guard took her out and carried her to the Hoop and Grapes Public House in Queen-square where every method that could be devised, was ineffectually exerted to restore animation.

She was very tall and beautiful, finely shaped, of a delicate skin, auburn hair, blue eyes. She was dressed in a muslin gown, chip hat, with a pink handkerchief about it, a red coral neck-lace with a gold locket, and silk stockings.

On the inquest, Mr. Whitrow informed the Coroner, that her name was Mary Champante; that he was the partner of the young lady's father; they keep a bookseller's shop in Jewry Street, Aldgate. The deceased was in her twenty-first year and was an amiable girl except that she was a little flighty at times, but nothing serious was apprehended from her flighty manner. Her mother had been subject to fits of insanity. On the morning of the day of the unfortunate affair, the deceased came from Chelsea with her sister. She wished to say something to her father, but he was busy and could not listen to her; she then said that she would go and destroy herself, but no person believed that she had any such intention. She told the clerk to call her a coach, but while he was gone for that purpose, she went out towards George-street, he believed, and got one for herself.

The Coroner wrote down the verdict — Deranged in her mind, and in a fit of insanity drowned herself.

A Private in the Shropshire Militia, having got a quantity of gun powder in a glass bottle, threw a little from the mouth of it into the fire with a view of alarming his wife; but the flash communicating with the contents of the bottle, the whole exploded, forcing a part of the glass into his breast, producing instant death.

A shocking accident happened a few days ago at Bridlington Quay, Yorkshire; as two little boys, the one seven, the other only two years of age, were at play in Mr. Sawdon's granary, along with some other children, the oldest having met with a loaded pistol in the yard, which Mr. Sawdon's servant had incautiously left there, after returning from shooting; he took it up, and in endeavouring to imitate the soldiers in their manoeuvres, not knowing it was loaded, the little child, his brother, called 'fire' and shot him dead on the spot.

Monday morning, a girl, about ten years of age, named Davis, nursing her brother, only two years old, near the Horseferry, Westminster, the infant crying very much, she threw it from her arms into the Thames, and ran away: but fortunately the transaction was observed by several persons, who secured the girl, and went to the assistance of the child, who sank twice; when taken out of the river, the usual methods were used to recall suspended animation, which was happily effected.

A few days since as John Ringer, aged twenty six, was attending the boulting mill, in a windmill belonging to Mr. Francis Bacon, of Dickleburgh, the cogs caught hold of his frock slop, and so entangled him, that he was carried round by the same for three hours, in which time he was reduced to a most horrid spectacle.

A singular and melancholy circumstance happened a few days ago in Salt-lane. A very fine child, two years of age, was sitting with his mother at dinner, when a boy, about twelve years, entered the house with a frightful old mask on his face; the sight of which so much alarmed the poor infant, that he fell into fits, in which he continued five or six days, and then died.

A Grocer in Holborn forbade his son to marry the daughter of a very respectable shopkeeper in Grays Inn road. Arguments on the question raged for two days, but the father was not to be moved. The son went to his room and shot himself, the ball entering his left cheek and passing through his brain. The Jury at the Coroner's Inquest brought in a verdict of Lunacy.

A beautiful and engaging young woman, of a respectable family, who unhappily listened to the seductive arts and persuasions of an officer, quitted her parents on his account, and resided some time in genteel lodgings, where her seducer left her unprotected, a prey to sickness and grief, for her fatal deviation from happy innocence. As soon as her health enabled her, she formed the resolution of returning home, hoping by penitence to atone for the sorrow she had occasioned to her parents; but they refusing to receive her, she went to an inn, and requesting a private room for a few minutes, the landlady left her, but soon returning, found the poor victim of a seduction a corpse.

A few days since two boys set fire to some loose grains lying on a cask of gunpowder in a store at Ashburton, in Devonshire, when the cask immediately exploded and blew up the store and an adjoining house. The boys, with a servant in the store, were blown to atoms.

Thursday morning W. Ash, T. Ash (father and son), W. Arnold and J. Fowler, shipwrights, were at work in the magazine of the BELLEROPHON, lying in dock, a candle (the place being secluded from the light) communicated itself to some loose powder, and they were in an instant rendered the most shocking spectacles by the effect of the explosion.

Miss S. Smith of Dorchester was alone one night at her brother-in-law's, C. Cozen's, when on fetching wood from the cellar, the muslin of her dress caught in the candle. She was burnt from the neck down. She survived some fourteen hours conscious enough to relate the events in spite of the pain.

Late on Saturday night, as Mr. Johnson, schoolmaster of Beccles and Mr. Goffe of Worlingham were returning home in a one horse chaise, in going over Beccles bridge, the horse took

fright and overturned the chaise, by which means Mr. Johnson
was killed on the spot and Mr. Goffe so much hurt as to render
his recovery hopeless.

On Tuesday morning an Excise Officer, named Littlejohn, was
found dead in a vat of strong beer, in a state of fermentation,
in the brewhouse of Mr. Thornton at Horsham. It came out in
evidence before the Coroner's Jury, on a view of the body, that
the deceased went into the brewhouse on Monday night to
make his accustomed survey, and that in leaning over the vessel,
the azotic gas arising from the beer in such a state might
suffocate him and cause him to fall into the liquor, they therefore returned a verdict of Accidental Death. The vessel contained about sixteen barrels of beer, which by Mr. Thornton's
directions was thrown into the common sewer.

Sunday, as the wife of John Brew, a watchman in Whitechapel,
was reading the Bible at the fireside, a spark flew from the fire

and set her clothes in a blaze; and before any assistance could be got, she was so miserably burned, that she languished until Monday and then expired.

On Tuesday se'nnight, a shocking circumstance occurred at Cottingham, near Hull. A woman having left a child a few months old, in the cradle, while she went out upon some occasion, and negligently omitted to shut the door, on her return found the child lying on the floor, and both its hands nearly eaten off by a sow which had got into the house.

The Barracks at Dorchester had, on Tuesday night, nearly been destroyed by fire, in consequence of some of the German Legion having retired to bed with their pipes in their mouths. They had fallen asleep, and the lighted tobacco having communicated to the bed cloaths, the whole ward was in a blaze before discovered.

Tuesday se'nnight, the Rev. Richard Bowden of Darwin in Lancashire, with a party of friends, returning from a neighbouring village at a late hour in the evening, had occasion to cross a brook suddenly swollen by the rains. They were on horseback; Mrs. Bowden proceeding foremost, her horse was by the force of the current thrown off his feet and the lady was carried down the stream and perished. Mr. Bowden leaping from his horse made a vain attempt to save her, and was himself, not without great difficulty, dragged out alive. The body of the unfortunate lady was not found till the next morning.

As the son of Mr. Norton, a boy of eight years of age, at school at Reigate in Surry, was crossing a stile, with the blade of a very small knife in his hand, he put it into his mouth, and in jumping down, swallowed it. The child, however, felt but little pain from the accident, and had not been at home many days before the sharp portion of steel passed his bowels and placed him out of all danger.

A few days since, the gardener of T. May, esq. of Littlebourn-court, Kent, incautiously threw the clippings of a yew tree into the farmyard where they were devoured by the hogs, and in a few hours after, thirty two of them dropped down dead.

Court and Social News and Entertainments

The prevailing colours in London are geranium, rose, blue and purple. The dresses continue to be made very low, and the sleeves quite plain with lace let in, lace tuckers drawn round the bosom. Pelisses of all colours are universally worn, but black velvet or light blue kerseymere are the most genteel.

Parisian Fashions.
The most fashionable flowers are daisies, more frequently white than coloured. The Tituses are out of fashion, and all the ladies appear to have long hair. A great many wear wigs or demi-wigs with flesh coloured stripes.

The Duchess of Marlborough gave a grand rout on Thursday night, at Marlborough-house, Pall Mall. We never saw so great a profusion of the most fragrant and beautiful shrubs and flowers, as were collected to adorn this very magnificent mansion. All the hot-houses and green-houses of Sion-hill were stripped of their sweets. Six waggons full of them arrived in town on Thursday; and taste and fancy were immediately set at work to dispose them to advantage in the various apartments. They consisted of orange and lemon trees, in full bearing, myrtles, roses, sweetbriars, pinks, cloves, carnations etc. of the rarest species.

A new and interesting FEMALE ASSOCIATION has been lately formed under the Patronage of Her Majesty and the Princesses, entitled THE LADIES COMMITTEE FOR PRO-MOTING THE EDUCATION AND EMPLOYMENT of the FEMALE POOR. In this distinguished list are the Dowager Marchioness of Donegal, Countess of Lonsdale, Countess Harcourt etc. A Treatise upon this Committee appeals to the *men milliners* and asks "Whether they would not handle a

Birmingham firelock better than Brussels lace, and feel more pleasure in pinning a Frenchman than a feather to a cap."

DRAWING ROOM. Her Majesty wore a bright orange coloured satin petticoat with a bordering of black velvet, with a rich silver fringe round the bottom, and a drapery of black velvet vandyked, trimmed round with a very rich Turkish halvine chains and tassels. An elegant turban and a sash of fine black lace looped up with silver rouleau, beautiful silver cords and tassels.

Her Royal Highness, the Princess of Wales, as usual displayed great taste, in the choice of her dress. Her petticoat was yellow velvet, entirely covered over in silver net; at the bottom of the petticoat was a most splendid embroidery to form wreaths and bunches of oak. The train, yellow velvet trimmed all around with silver fringe which had a very brilliant effect. It was entirely different from anything of the kind we have yet seen. The head-dress was extremely beautiful, diamonds in great abundance, tastefully displayed.

First Subscription Assembly for 1804 at Assembly Rooms, Thursday 26, January.

Admittance to non-subscribers not living in Ipswich or within six miles thereof; Ladies 5/- Gentlemen 10/6 Supper and wine included.

The Public are respectfully acquainted that it is intended to perform the Oratorio of the MESSIAH and JUDAS MACCA-BAEUS, in the Church of Great Yarmouth, some time in the middle of August. The whole will be under the direction of Mr. Eager and Dr. Beckwith, and the principal Vocal and instrumental parts will be supported by Gentlemen who have obligingly complied with Mr. Eager's request, to assist in the performance. The Band will also comprehend such professional talents as will render it in every respect complete. Four Transferable Tickets, admitting 2 persons to each Oratorio, will be issued to Subscribers at 12/- Non-subscribers 4/- each.

NEWMARKET. The prevailing colours are lilac, green and yellow. Straw hats of the Spanish shape, plain or ornamented with flowers.

Mrs. Massey is said to have eloped from the Marquis of Headford, with an Officer of the Guards. The Marquis, on carrying her from her husband, settled on her 1200£ a year.

CAROLINE de MANEVILLE. This was an infant of the age of eight months, who was brought into Court under a Habeas Corpus directed to Louis de Maneville, her father. The question before the Court, was Caroline to remain in the care of her father or mother or whether the jurisdiction of the Court could be extended so far as to deprive the male parent of the custody of his own child? Affadavits from the highest military characters in the country with whom this Gentleman had fought side by side in the Army of the Royalists were called.

Messrs. Eskine, Garrow & Gibbs, spoke of the great barbarity of this foreigner (who was an Alien) to the young woman of family and fortune whom he had married. They represented the probability that he would take the infant to a foreign country and deprive it of the sustenance and consolation the mother alone could afford it.

Lord Ellenborough said the father is entitled to possession of his child.

The friends of the Young Roscius are determined that he shall make a good market of his talents while the novelty lasts. A treaty has been opened between them and the Drury Lane

Managers, and it is said that the terms required are no less than 50£ a night, for 12 performances, and a free benefit. Earl Moira, we understand has been very liberal in his patronage of this embryo Garrick.

A Grand Masquerade was given at Woburn Mansion, by her Grace the Duchess of Bedford, to which nearly 150 persons of distinction were invited; they assembled as early as 8 o'clock. The major part of the company were in dominos, though we noticed several well supported characters, particularly the Duchess of Bedford, as a House Maid, which she supported to admiration; his Grace the Duke of Bedford as John Bull, or Farmer, which he supported with much humour, and added greatly to the entertainment of the evening; and Mr. Sheridan, as a Fishwoman, who delivered upon the occasion an appropriate speech, and kept them in a continual roar. There were also several Harlequins, Indian Chiefs, Flower Girls, Millers, Chimney Sweepers, Dustmen etc. At 9 o'clock the ball commenced with Speed the Plough. The ballroom was superbly decorated with wreaths of artificial flowers and variegated lamps; in the middle of the room hung 5 most elegant chandeliers; the floor was beautifully chalked, and exhibited a most charming coup d'oeil. At half past one o'clock the supper-rooms were thrown open; the tables were covered with every delicacy that ingenuity could invent or the season afford. The wines and desserts were of the choicest.

Mrs. Thellusson's MASQUERADE on Thursday night at Foley House, if possible, exceeded all the former ones. About 1100 persons were present, all of whom, (with the exception of a very few) were in character dresses. The entrance into the court-yard of Foley house was illuminated by variegated lamps, and over the garden gate, on the North side, was placed a brilliant star of uncommon magnitude, which was intended as a guide to the masks (after their tickets had been inspected) where to enter into the scene of mirth and gaiety. Passing through this gate, the eye was attracted and the footsteps were directed by numerous arches of variegated lamps placed from tree to tree across the public walk. Turning the angle on the right, the whole scene opened itself to view. In the front, opposite the Northern side of Foley House, was erected a stage of about 30ft. square and 12ft. high, supported by six poles, each of which was nearly 40ft. long covered with green boughs and surrounded by variegated lamps. The walk which leads to the gallery and from thence through the ballroom into the house, (all other doors being locked) was lighted with lamps. Over the gallery an awning was erected as a security against bad weather; this precaution proved wholly unnecessary, the night being very fine. Branches of trees of the most beautiful foliage, entwined with variegated lamps, were placed around the columns which supported the roof. The same kind of ornaments were affixed to the wall, and festoons of lamps were placed across every window, which had a very pleasing effect.

About 11 o'clock the masks began to arrive; at 12, the throng was so great that it was almost impossible to examine the tickets with that degree of celerity the impatient owners required. The press at that hour was owing to a notice written on the back of each ticket, that none would be admitted after half past twelve o'clock. From 11 till one the company danced to the excellent band of Messrs. Gow and a Military Band played at intervals soft music in the garden.

A dramatic piece called The Emperor of the Gulls, in ridicule of Bonaparte, was withdrawn, at the pressing solicitation of the Prince, and a noble Marquis (having a son in France whose safety, as well as that of the other English prisoners, it was thought might be endangered by its mock heroic representation.)

About 2 o'clock Mr. Thellusson ushered the motley group into the grand hall, where a platform had been erected with scenery, composed of clouds etc. Here her Grace, the Duchess of Leeds, the Miss Anguishes, Mr. Spencer etc. appeared as gods and goddesses, and sung several charming airs in Italian and

English, with great science and effect. This novel species of amusement lasted three quarters of an hour, when the seven supper rooms were thrown open, and displayed a magnificent banquet, with covers laid for 740 persons. The Prince of Wales, Dukes of Cambridge and Cumberland, Prince William of Gloucester, Duchess of Devonshire etc etc. 32 in number, supped in a private room adjoining the ballroom. The supper was cold, and consisted of every delicacy, the company did not depart till 6 o'clock.

MR. JONAS
Who has had the Honor to perform with the greatest satisfaction before Their Majesties and the Royal Family
at Frogmore Lodge.
Will display his much admired
PHILOSOPHIC EXPERIMENTS
In the Assembly Room, Ipswich
on Saturday and Monday evenings 4 & 6 August.

On Monday, 31 Dec. there will be a Farmers' and Tradesmen's Ball at the White Hart Inn, Stowmarket. Tickets for a Gentleman & Lady 3/6, tea, coffee etc. included; and if a second lady is introduced to pay 2/6 extra.
Proper Stewards appointed.

The Entertainment of CINDERELLA, which has been a considerable time in preparation, and has excited much the curiosity of the town, was on Tuesday night brought forward at Drury Lane Theatre, before an audience the most numerous of the season. The dances are allegorical, and intended to illustrate the powers and attributes of beauty, the graces, love and marriage. Independent of the mythological introduction, which is infinitely too tedious, the tale of Cinderella is told to the following effect: Her two Sisters in sumptuous attire are preparing for the ball, at which the poor cinder wench is unfit to attend, till, by the intervention of a magical power, recognized in the fables of infancy, her dress from the depth of misery is changed to the extremity of splendour, a chariot embossed with jewels is produced from a gourd, and six rats caught in a trap, are, by a touch of the wand, metamorphosed into cream coloured horses, bitted and caparisoned. Cinderella is admonished not to remain at the ball longer than twelve, but heedless of the time, she permits the period to elapse, and at length, escapes with the loss of her little glass slipper, which the Prince, who is enamoured of her, preserves, and discovering her by its peculiar conformation to her foot, the piece concluded with the mortification of her sisters and the nuptials of Cinderella.

The receipts of Sheffield Theatre during performances of the Young Roscius's fourteen nights are stated to amount to £1469.3s. At the Liverpool last week, he brought 900£ by three performances, of which sum a third was his share.

It is a fact that to a gentleman who possessed eight box tickets, for the Manchester Theatre on Monday evening, when Young Roscius was to perform the part of Frederick in Lovers Vows, 16 gns. were offered to resign them, which he refused.

The Duchess of Devonshire, while waiting in her carriage one day in the streets of London, observed a dustman, with a short pipe in his hand, looking at her. Having gazed a few seconds with intenseness, he broke into a smile and said, "Lord love your Ladyship, I wish you would let me light my pipe at your eyes!" Her Grace took it in good part, and was so pleased with the whimsical frankness of the compliment, that when anything civil is said to her, she often remarks, "Very well; but nothing like the dustman."

LORD NELSON'S HEALTH has been for some time in a
delicate state; but the most alarming of his complaints is a
diminishing of sight in his remaining eye.

Adjoining the Churchyard, Hadleigh
Never Displayed Here
On Monday, Wednesday & Thursday Evening, Mr. Lloyd
from London, will deliver his Course of Astronomical Lectures,
illustrated by the New
DIOASTRODOXON
or Grand Transparent Orrery
Twenty-one feet diameter
When every embellishment the Science can receive from
impressive Classic Beauty in progressive change will be introduced.
    This Course will embrace a variety of new and interesting
matter, rarely given in Public Lectures, forming a grateful
repast for the Gentleman, the Scholar, and the Man of Business.

The liberality of the above arrangements, and the supremacy of the apparatus, is universally acknowledged by the first ranks of enlightened society in the United Kingdom.

Non-subscribers 3/6 each lecture. To begin at 7 o'clock. Subscriptions are received by Mr. Leatherdale, bookseller, of whom may be had, a Companion to the Course, price 6d.

On Valentine's Day, the Twopenny Post had such an extraordinary influx of letters with Valentines from the lads and the lasses, that the postmen, altho' assisted by a number of supernumeraries, could not get through their deliveries in the regular time. At the receiving house in New-street, Covent Garden, near 1000 Valentine's were put into the box.

Brighton is now so completely filled with company that beds are not to be procured at any price. Many of the visitants on Friday night were obliged to leave the place, in consequence; while others were content to seek repose, not only on sofas etc. but even the haylofts had a proportional share of guests. The Prince arrived at the Pavilion about 11 p.m. An assemblage so numerous and brilliant as the race hill displayed that day was never seen in that part of the world before.

Amongst the equestrians on the ground were, the Earl of Egremont, the Nestor of the Turf, Earl of Clermont, Lord Craven, Sir T.C. Bunbury etc.

Mr. Le Gros from the Opera House, begs leave to inform the Military Families residing in Colchester, that he intends opening a DANCING ACADEMY for YOUNG LADIES on 1, August. Families who will favour him with their patronage, are requested to apply to:
Mr. Le Gros, East Hill, Colchester.
Schools attended in the Country.

There are now exhibiting at the Principal Towns of Suffolk and
Norfolk, Three of the greatest PHOENOMENA of NATURE,
ever exhibited to the Public. If we turn over the whole of
animated nature we shall not find anything to excite our
astonishment so much as that

WONDERFUL MAN — THE SPOTTED INDIAN

born of parents in Jamaica; his head is covered with black and
white wool, his breast, arms and legs are of a delicate white,
equal to any European, spotted and intermixed with black,
resembling a beautiful leopard; in short, it is impossible to
give human imagination an idea of so matchless a curiosity; he
imitates various kinds of birds, particularly the skylark, thrush,
blackbird, nightingale, etc. also the young pig, puppy, etc. also

THE PATAGONIAN YOUTH

from South America, this Gigantic Youth stands nearly 8 feet
high, only 25 years of age, is well proportioned and is astonish-
ing to all beholders.

Likewise THE SURPRISING LITTLE MAN

only 36 inches high, 24 years of age, he will go through the
Broad Sword Exercise in a most correct manner.

Admittance 1/- Children etc. 6d.

The Young Roscius.

At the Theatre in Stockport he received 60 gns. Prices of boxes
rose from 3/- to 7/-.

The doors opened at 11 a.m. for the Play to begin at 12. Such
was the clamour that the Young Roscius at very short notice
agreed to appear that same evening as Richard III.

When Cooke, on Tuesday night, while Playing Richard, read the
paper containing the words,

> "Jockey of Norfolk, be not too bold
>
> For Dickey, thy master is bought and sold —"

all eyes were turned upon his Grace the Duke of Norfolk,
who sat in one of the front boxes. Some did not scruple even to

burst into a loud laugh, in which his Grace very good humouredly joined.

Monday, being the NATAL DAY of our BELOVED SOVEREIGN, was ushered in with the usual solemnities. At one o'clock 66 guns were fired from the Park, and as many from the Tower in honour of the day, and to denote the number of years which His Majesty has completed.

The opinion of his physicians was, that the fatigue of the Drawing Room might be injurious to his health in his present precarious state of convalescence. The cheering aspect of the Queen, of her Royal daughters, of the Princess of Wales and of the Duchess of York, left no doubt in the minds of the splendid assemblage, that the non appearance of His Majesty was owing rather to a wise precaution than to absolute necessity.

About three quarters past 12 o'clock the Queen and members of the Royal Family, appeared at the windows near the private entrance of the Royal Family (at St. James's Palace) to gratify the curiosity of the numerous populace.

The company began to arrive at the palace soon after 12 o'clock, but the Drawing-room being expected to be extremely crowded, and the heat of the weather excessive, the Lord Chamberlain gave orders that the doors of the Council Chamber, where the Drawing-room is held, should not be opened till Her Majesty was ready to enter it, for the purpose of keeping it as cool as possible. On account of this regulation, the company continued coming even till every avenue leading to the room, even to the bottom of the principal staircase, was so crowded, and the heat was so great, that several ladies fainted, and some of the female spectators were carried out apparently lifeless. At half past two, Her Majesty and the Royal Family entered the centre door, and their entrance was announced by the Earl of Dartmouth (as Lord Chamberlain) by the waving of his wand of office.

Music was played, by command of His Majesty from the works of Handel. An ode was given by H.J. Pye.

Her Majesty wore a blue sarsnet petticoat, entirely covered with Turkish silver net, superb fringe and tassels, chain bordering the bottom, finishing with silver shell work, stripes of brilliant laurel wreaths closing each wave of net, very rich balloon acorns, silver tassels with silver bows; the mantle rich blue silver tissue, trimmed with imperial silver fringe. Head-dress blue sarsnet cap, richly spangled with silver and ornamented with a profusion of diamonds.

The Princess of Wales had one of the most superb dresses ever exhibited even at Court. The ground was white with yellow drapery; the festoons and other appendages were rich beyond description.

H.R.H. the Duchess of York wore a superb rich petticoat embroidered in draperies, Mosaic pattern, relieved by rich spangled stripes and drawn up with rich silver tassels and wreaths of green vine leaves, entwined round the bottom, robe dark green and silver gown, the sleeves ornamented with lace and a profusion of diamonds, head-dress was a tiara of diamonds and rubies and fine white ostrich feathers.

Princess Sophia of Gloucester wore a blue and silver gauze petticoat ornamented at the bottom with vandykes of silver; a spangled silver net drapery, bordered with pointed fringe and tassels, the effect of which was new and very elegant; wreaths of silver cord and superb tassels, ornamented on the left side of the petticoat with blue and silver; train richly trimmed with silver; net sleeves, trimmed with net to correspond with the drapery.

The company had not left the Palace till 7 o'clock. They were prevented from returning for several hours, by the improper conduct of the Military on duty, who took the management into their own hands, and put the civil power at defiance. Townsend, the Police Officer, was wounded in his left arm by a bayonet; several genteel females were wounded, some with bayonets, and some with the butt ends of muskets; several livery servants received wounds while waiting for their masters and mistresses, and were all turned out of the Court-Yard, where it has always been customary for them to attend.

At the Theatre in Drury Lane on Tuesday, Miss Duncan made her first appearance as Lady Teazle in SCHOOL for SCANDAL. In the coaxing, the sarcastic, and the penitentially pathetic parts of the dialogue, she entered into the character with great correctness and felicity of imitation and the audience were highly pleased.

Monday night, at Covent Garden Theatre, Mr. Cooke, who was to play the Ghost in HAMLET was overtaken by some *evil spirits. Alas, poor Ghost!* In the first scene of his appearance, articulation refused its aid, and the solemn talk was lost in very irregular and unsteady motion. The audience soon perceived the cause of this falling off, and assailed him with a storm of hisses, shouts of 'Off, Off' issued from every part of the house, with all the horrible noises that can be imagined. For a long time he braved the pelting of the pitiless storm, but was at length obliged to yield to its overwhelming force. Mr. Kemble, in Hamlet, exerted himself in an extraordinary degree, to make amends for his deficiency and was received with thunders of applause. Mr. Cooke thought himself sufficiently recovered to attempt the last scene of the Ghost, and accordingly presented himself, but the audience would not suffer him to speak and he was obliged again to retire.

Theatre Halesworth — By Desire of the Officers & Gentlemen of the 8th Troop of Loyal Suffolk Yeomanry, this evening, Sat. Oct. 13, Fisher & Scraggs Company will perform the Comedy of JOHN BULL and Love Laughs at Locksmiths.
On Tuesday, The Heir at Law and The Paragraph
Wednesday, By Desire etc. of the Halesworth Loyal Volunteers the Comedy of THE POOR GENTLEMAN and the Review THE WAGS OF WINDSOR. Friday, By Desire of Lord and Lady Huntingfield the Musical Drama THE WIFE OF TWO HUSBANDS and RAISING THE WIND

On Saturday for the last time The Nouvelle Exhibition of
PHANTASMORGARIA after which other Entertainments.
On Tuesday a Play and Farce For the Benefit of Mr. & Mrs.
Fisher. To begin at half past Five o'clock.

Friday morning about 9 o'clock, the Royal Family and
attendants left Windsor Lodge. The King and Queen arrived at
Salisbury in his post chaise, exactly at ten minutes after 12 that
night. The Salisbury Volunteers, commanded by Col. Bouchier,
and a detachment of the Wiltshire Yeomanry, commanded by
Lord Bruce, were drawn up opposite the White Hart Inn, where
the Royal carriages stopped to receive them. Neither the King
nor the Queen alighted. The King let down the left hand glass,
the side on which he sat, and seeing the Salisbury Volunteers
receive him with their colours and presented arms, called Major
General Head to him and asked the strength of the corps, and
said, "I am sorry to have occasioned their being turned out at so
late an hour." He was received with loyal acclamations by the
populace.

The Princesses followed immediately in a post coach and
four, under an escort of Dragoons. Flags were displayed on all
the church steeples, and the bells rung the whole day. Having
exchanged their post horses, which were driven by the King's
postillions, they set off in less than five minutes for Blandford,
under an escort of the Prince's (10th) Light Dragoons, which
were to be relieved by another detachment of the same
regiment, to proceed with their Majesties to Weymouth.

Saturday morning about 5, their Majesties, the Princesses
Augusta, Elizabeth and Sophia, arrived at the King's Lodge
there, to the great joy of the inhabitants who were anxiously
waiting in great crowds for their arrival, and received the Royal
Family with acclamations and every demonstration of joy. The
Royal Family went to bed immediately on their arrival. His
Majesty got up soon after 7, and after breakfast walked on the
Esplanade for a considerable time.

It is stated in the fashionable circles, that Her Majesty has determined to dispose of her elegant house in St. James's Park, with all the appurtenances, including the whole garden, riding house, outhouses, improvements, etc. from Buckingham-gate to Hyde Park Corner.

H.R.H. the Princess of Wales, we are much concerned to state, met with a very serious accident on Friday last. In the morning she paid a visit in the neighbourhood of Charlton. When the visit was over, H.R. Highness had taken her seat in her carriage. she waved her hand in farewell salutation of her friends; at this moment, the footman, who attended the door of the carriage, closed it with great violence. Unfortunately, the fingers of Her Royal Highness's right hand were caught between the door and the pannel, and mangled in a miserable manner. She gave a piercing shriek, and the Ladies, whom she was in the act of saluting, flew to the carriage. On opening the door, the four fingers were found almost severed from the hand in a most shocking condition; the nail of one had been torn off, and was found sticking to the door. Medical assistance was immediately procured and the hand dressed. Her Royal Highness has been ever since in the most excruciating pain; but we are happy to add, that the surgeons in attendance do not conceive that the amputation of any of the fingers will be necessary.

From Weymouth, Sept. 6.
About 10 o'clock, their Majesties, the Princesses, Duke of Cambridge, and all the General Officers, Lords Hawkesbury, Uxbridge, Paulet and Hinton, Ladies Wynyard, Thynne, Ilchester and Spencer and Mrs. Drake, left the Lodge for the Royal barge, which was waiting to convey them to the Island of Portland. The barge had a royal standard at her stern, and an awning of beautiful silk large enough to cover the whole company. The Royal Family were surrounded by boats for many hundred yards, and the ships in the harbour fired a royal salute as they

passed. Vast numbers of people, who could not get boats, were on the hills and coast, facing Portland, huzzaing, singing 'God Save the King' and shewing every possible demonstration of joy. Great preparations have been making for several days past at Portland Castle for the entertainment of the Royal Family.

H.R.H. the Princess of Wales, we are happy to say, was much better on Wednesday and is not likely to suffer any permanent injury from her late accident. H.R.H. being informed that the footman, who had closed the carriage door upon her hand, had absented himself and was exceedingly distressed in his mind in consequence of the misfortune, desired, with her characteristic kindness and benevolence, that he should return to his duty, as it was a mere accident, and no blame could attach to him.

At Weymouth on Saturday, the anniversary of the Coronation was celebrated, among other festivities, by a magnificent entertainment at the Royal Hotel, at which were present more than 100 persons of rank and fashion, upon invitation from their Majesties. Dances began soon after dinner, and with the interruption only of tea and other refreshments were continued until 11 o'clock at night.

Master Betty — better known as the Young Roscius, will, we are told, play at Covent Garden theatre for the first time next Tuesday fortnight.

Young Roscius was at Drury Lane Theatre on Wednesday night in one of the lower private boxes, near the top of the pit. He was not long unobserved, and the eager curiosity of the few, who were near him, soon communicated itself to others in distant parts of the house. In the intervals of the performance, the seats in the lower part of the pit were deserted, and the upper part was crowded with persons endeavouring to look from them into the box where he sat. In the boxes, the same eagerness was shewn; the ladies in those immediately over his, leaned over to obtain a peep at him; from every quarter of the house all eyes were directed towards the same spot, though but few could reach over the front of his box. Many persons left the theatre, and stationed themselves near the entrance to the private boxes, that they might see him, as he came out. He stayed the whole play, sitting behind two ladies and apparently very merry with them and his father at the extraordinary attention he had excited. His appearance is still more juvenile than we had expected; his dress that of a child, with an open shirt collar spread upon his shoulders.

The Young Roscius.
The first appearance of Master Betty before a London audience, on Saturday evening at Covent Garden Theatre, may be considered as a remarkable epoch in the history of the English stage. To see a boy who has barely attained his thirteenth year,

perform some of the most difficult characters in the British
Drama, not with the mere endurance, but with the vehement
and tumultuary applause of crowded and critical audiences, is
a circumstance, so much above common credulity, that we
require the evidence of our eyes and ears to be satisfied of the
fact. The extraordinary reputation which has followed the
theatrical exertions of Master Betty at the different provincial
theatres has been the harbinger of his appearance in the metropolis; and it was to be expected that the public curiosity would
have been proportionate to the professional fame he had
acquired. On no occasion has there been a stronger and more
ardent desire manifested by all ranks and descriptions of people
to gain admittance to the Theatre. So early as 10 a.m. on
Saturday morning, many gentlemen began to parade the Piazzas
and Bow Street, in order that they might be near the doors
when the crowd should begin to assemble. So early as 12
o'clock numbers had taken their stations near all the doors leading to the pit, boxes and galleries; long before the doors were
opened, they stretched out in long, thick, close-wedged, impenetrable columns, to the extremity of the Piazzas, in Covent
Garden and quite across Bow Street. Many who did not mean to

attempt to get in, lined the streets and windows, contemplating with sentiments of awe and fear the tremendous accumulation of numbers. In the crowd before the doors, long before they were opened, the heat and pressure became so intolerable that many persons fainted, and others were in danger of suffocation from the weight and force of the numbers without. The danger at last was so great, that the guards were unanimously called for by the terrified persons who were included between the inner and outer doors and who could not make good their retreat. The soldiers after some time appeared and with the utmost dexterity, and good temper cleared the crowd from without; and their lining the entrance permitted everyone to retire but no one to enter.

As the numbers were so great, the doors were opened about half an hour before the usual time. The rush was terrific at all the doors leading to the body of the house. In the space of a few minutes the two galleries were filled, so closely wedged that not one more could get admittance. The pit was two thirds filled, not from the pit doors and passages, but from the boxes. Gentlemen who knew there were no places untaken in the boxes, and who could not get up in the pit avenue paid for admission to the boxes, and poured from the front boxes into the pit in twenties and thirties at a time. Still, even after it was crammed, the gentlemen crowded the front boxes, and being unable, for want of room, to descend to the pit, remained there. It was in vain that those who had taken them, perhaps weeks before, attempted to get to their places, some ladies however, were suffered to occupy the front rows. The police officers fruitlessly attempted to clear the other rows, but the first occupants remained the permanent possessors. The heat within was intense, there was a complete lack of air and everywhere ladies were endeavouring to keep themselves and their neighbours cool by the urgent use of fans. Screams were heard on all sides as those overcome by the heat and unable to move succumbed to insensiblity. The press of the throng was so great that the pickpockets amongst them were soon detected as they were unable to get away.

When Kemble appeared and attempted to make an occasional address the clamour and uproar from the audience was such that he was forced to retire. The Play started, but the audience was interested only in the Young Roscius and gave a noisy reception to the other actors, but a deathly hush fell prior to his entrance which was then greeted with a thunder of applause; the Young Roscius bowed but his self possession did not appear shaken. His voice faltered at first. He appeared dressed as the slave Achmet in white linen pantaloons, a short close, russet jacket trimmed with sable, with a turban hat. His countenance is prepossessing, his eye quick, intelligent and expressive. His mouth is pleasing, his figure well made, and rather taller than boys of thirteen usually are. If he felt embarrassment at his entry, it vanished in a few minutes and immediately he was the actor. The emphasis which he lay on certain words, his tender expression, the softened subdued, pathetic tone in which he spoke the word 'Mother' touched every heart. He received from some ladies the flattering tribute of their tears, while others not content to applaud with hands and feet, mounted the benches and threw up their hats in loud huzzas.

The Prince of Wales was present in Lady Melbourne's box. Some ladies stood behind the scenes that they might get a better view of him. As to his acting it must be said that when he had finished his speeches he did not drop into that vacuity of stare, that want of expressive looks, that wandering gaze which roams round the house, and is directed everywhere but where it ought, which are so common in most of our actors. He pleased as much when silent as when he spoke. Full of grace and ease, every limb, every gesture conspire to give effect to the emotions of his soul; and he seems not a mere human being acting under the influence of ordinary reason but governed by a wonderful instinct, and by the magical inspiration of genius.

The father of the Young Roscius has vested in the hands of respectable trustees (himself being one) the profits arising from his son's talents. The whole amount of 6000£ has been converted into 3% Stock. This completely rebuts the illiberal insinuations which have been circulated on this subject.

A Miss Fisher, who has appeared with much eclat at Richmond, in the part of Richard III, is, it is said, engaged at the rate of 15£ per week for Drury Lane Theatre where she is to make her debut when Master Betty's engagement closes.

In consequence of H.M's determination no longer to reside at the Queen's House in the Park, but to remain altogether at Windsor Castle, those who have apartments at Windsor Castle, including the Prince of Wales and other Princes, have been desired to remove, as their apartments will in future be required for the accommodation of His Majesty's family. Orders have been given, it is added, to remove the Royal Library, one of the finest in the country, and everything connected with the convenience of pleasure of His Majesty's residence at Windsor, from the Queen's House in the Park.

Letter from Bridport.
As the Royal Family were returning on Thursday from their visit to the Earl of Uxbridge, on their way back to Milton Abbey, in passing up a very steep hill two of the horses in a phaeton, in which were two of the Princesses, got entangled together, which caused the phaeton to overset; the Princesses were of course thrown out, but we are extremely happy to say they received no bodily injury, they were very much frightened.

His Majesty has purchased Dr. Heberden's house at Windsor and is fitting it up for the Princess Charlotte of Wales in order to have her near him.

Every room set apart for the Royal Family at Windsor, is fitted up in the modern taste, the walls being painted a bright yellow, bordered with very rich groups of flowers of yellow and brown colours. The curtains are likewise yellow, made of silk, finished with French draperies and yellow and brown tassels. All the King's apartments are crowded with valuable paintings, removed principally from Buckingham House and Hampton Court.

The long expected interview between the Sovereign and the Heir Apparent took place on Monday, at Kew Palace. The Queen and the greater part of the Royal Family were present. The meeting of those two Personages, after a long interval, was marked, it is understood, by every emotion of kindness and conciliation on the one part, and of affectionate respect on the other. The scene is said to have been affecting beyond all description, and we are fully persuaded that the circumstance will afford the highest gratification to every loyal and feeling breast in the united realm.

As His Majesty intends passing almost the whole of the season in the Castle at Windsor, the following journal of the regular routine of the manner in which the Royal Family pass the day may not be deemed unacceptable. The King, who was always remarkable for being an early riser, is up and regularly between 5 and 6, walks to the Round Tower, where the workmen are employed or to view his stud of horses. Precisely at 7, H.M. breakfasts in his study alone, agreeably to his usual custom; at 8, goes to Chapel with one of the Princesses, either Elizabeth or Mary; at 9, the Queen and the Princesses breakfast together; 10-12 the King and Sophia and Amelia ride out on horseback if the weather proves favourable; at one His Majesty dines, an hour from which he has not deviated for the last 12 months, and the dinner consists of three courses. H.M.'s favourite beverage at table is a liquor called cup, made of Madeira, lemon and water. After dinner H.M. attends to business till 3, when the hour of dressing arrives. The Queen and the Princesses return from their morning's ride in their carriage about two when they dress for dinner. The Queen's hour is usually four. The King joins his family about 5 and takes coffee with them. The King retires to his study about 6 and again meets his family about 8 in the music room, adjoining to which the Queen's band plays. Sometimes the Princess Sophia plays on the new patent piano-forte and occasionally Amelia, Augusta and Mary; they all excel on that favourite instrument. The King has been known to play with a considerable degree of science, and the Duke of Sussex, who has composed several very sweet Italian airs, plays admirably well on the violon-cello. His Majesty, who is extremely fond of Handel's music, always has one or two pieces performed in the course of the evening. In this social and pleasant manner, the Royal Family pass their time until 10 o'clock, when supper takes place and at 11, the party separates to retire to rest.

Advertisements

Extraordinary Effects of Dr. JAMES'S FEVER POWDER. The very great Efficacy of this Medicine in the Influenza of last Year is too recent to be forgotten, but it was most singular when taken on the first attack, for in those cases, where the fever was allowed to gain ground and ravage the constitution, before the powder was resorted to, the disorder became obstinate, protracted and sometimes fatal. Upon all occasions this medicine should be given at the commencement of a fever, of whatever kind; for if it be not sufficient of itself to effect a cure, it is the best preparative for the bark and other remedies which the symptoms require; but as the genuine Powder has been often known to restore the patient, after its substitutes and every other febrifuge have failed, it ought even in the last extremity to be tried. Great benefits have been derived from the powder, when taken every night as an alternative, in disorders thought beyond the reach of medicine; and from a communication from the Rev. Mr. Singleton Harpur of Dublin, there is reason to believe that it may be used in this manner with success in the hydrocephalus or water on the brain. For colds, measles, rheumatisms, and all inflammations and obstructions of the lungs, bowels, etc, no medicine is so proper.

Packets 2s 9d (duty included) Bottles containing 12 packets 24s. as made up for the Army and Navy.

ABSTERGENT LOTION
For the Cure of Redness, Pimples, Blotches, Coarseness etc. in the face, hands and neck. 1 pint, 5s 5d. ½ pint, 2s. 9d. "Is warranted absolutely to remove without pain or trouble every kind of eruption in the Human Body, from whatsoever cause arising."

Samuel Berry's PALM SOPE
"is esteemed a valuable discovery for softening, cleansing, bracing and preserving the skin from the heat of the sun, and is found an excellent defence against cold winds and sharp frosty air."

Sold in balls and squares, 1s. each with the words Samuel Berry on the wrapper.

The proprietor recommends it as the best sope for gentlemen's shaving, producing a fine soft lather, proper for tender faces.

"The Poor Girl whom I recommended to you a few months ago, having derived great benefit from the use of your valuable Pills, desires to thank you for your kindness in giving them to her; she had been a long time indisposed, and had tried various things for her recovery, but nothing did her any service till she used your valuable medicine. She has been at service three months, but has now a relapse, and is afraid she must leave her place, unless you will have the goodness to give her another box, as she is a poor orphan, one of four, and she will humbly thank you for your goodness and you will much oblige your humble servant . . . . J. Matthews." 2s.9d a box.

S. Crawcour, Dentist, No. 15, Strand, London (Now at Mr. Shave's, St. Peter's, Ipswich.)
Begs leave to acquaint the Public at large, that owing to his numerous engagements, he has protracted his stay till the 15, July. He performs every operation for the preservation of the Teeth and Gums, assists children in removing their milk teeth at a proper season, lest they should turn their succeeding ones into a deformed state, as they are apt to grow double, which makes the lips appear thick, hurts the tongue, and affects the speech. When such an opportunity presents itself to the public, he hopes none will omit embracing the offer, who stand in need of his assistance.

Mr. Crawcour has made a remark how little value some people put on their teeth in the present age; how valuable they were in former time is illustrated by the following quotation; Exodus XXI, 27, "If a master smite out his slave servant's tooth, he shall let him go free for his tooth's sake," whom otherwise he would be obliged to serve for his life. Now the question is, what is the value of his slave servant which may be proved in verse 32 of the said chapter, "If a master loses his servant by the goring of an ox, he shall receive from the owner of the ox thirty shekels of silver (12£ English money) by which means the master was paid for the loss of his slave servant; but by smiting out his tooth he loses his slave servant, and gets nothing. Now as the slave servant's tooth is of so much value, how much more value must we esteem the free servant's or master's tooth?

N.B. Crawcour's Dentrifice Powder and Tincture to prevent the teeth from aching or decaying, which is much superior to any offered to the public, may be had from him as above, and from Messrs. Harmer and Green, and Mr. Bransby, Ipswich.

Newton's Dentifrice.
Patronised by their Majesties.
Royal Sweet Scented Lupin Soap for the much admired silky skin of oriental ladies.

Beauty and Cleanliness — to sweeten the Breath, cleanse the mouth, preserve and whiten the teeth, cure gum boils and remove all offensive Ulcerations.

AMBOYNA LOTION

The Drug from which the lotion is prepared was first imported by a gentleman of known character and fortune who having experienced its wonderful effects introduced it for the benefit of others. Nothing is so great a drawback to beauty as bad teeth, nothing more offensive than a foetid breath.

The lotion on the first application, improves the former and removes the latter, while by its antiputrescent and balsmic qualities prevents decay and removes all excrescences.

Dr. Arnold's Pills, celebrated for their superior efficacy and peculiar mildness, in perfectly eradicating every degree of the

Venereal Disease, without the least trouble or confinement. Full and plain directions are enclosed in each box, which will enable all persons to cure themselves, without the knowledge of anyone. 2s. 9d. a box.

East India Oils for Cuts Bruises, Sprains, Burns & Scalds, for use of Human Species. It is also an excellent remedy for Chilblains and has the same effect on all kinds of cattle. 1/- a Bottle.

Dr. Sibly's REANIMATING SOLAR TINCTURE
Sir, Mr. John Swan, a resident of Swansea, called at my shop and purchased two bottles of Solar Tincture and having received great benefit from taking it, being snatched, as it were from the jaws of death, he begged I would inform you of his case, for the benefit of the public in general. His complaint originated in a dreadful fever which left an inflammation on his lungs, and this not being removed in time, his lungs were ulcerated, and in that fatal situation, baffling all medical skill, he remained, till being advised by a friend (who had also received benefit in a similar complaint) to make trial of your inestimable medicine. And although reduced almost to a skeleton, he assured me he never enjoyed a better state of health than he does at present.
7s.6d. and 13s.0d. a bottle.

ABERCROMBIE'S EVERYMAN HIS OWN GARDENER or Pocket Journal being the daily assistant in the modern practice of English Gardening.

LONDON POST COACH — THE VOLUNTEER
Ipswich - London   1£ 6s.
Outside   15/-
Leaves Woodbridge 5 a.m. Arrives Charing Cross 6 p.m.

ART OF ANGLING IMPROVED   2/- sewn, 2/6 bound
Plate, representing the various flies.
A concise treatise on the Art of Angling confirmed by actual experience; interspersed with several new and recent discoveries: the whole forming a complete museum for the lovers of that pleasing and rational recreation.

Schwieppe's Soda and Seltzer Waters.

True Indian Nankeen Dye, which restores the lost colour to nankeens, and will dye muslins, cottons etc. of a beautiful buff hue.

The Genuine Patent SPILSBURY'S DROPS are only to be had with a black stamp; any offered with a red are counterfeits. Spilsbury's Patent Drops are excellent antidotes to Scurvy, Gout and Rheumatisms, as a numerous list of cures exemplify.
The Faculty recommend them in all scrophulous cases, in obstructions of the bowels caused by the morbid state of the misenteric glands, or in bilious cases, where the liver and bile vessels are incapable of supplying the proper quantity for use in the intestines.

GOOD NEWS
A Comfort to Mankind is in the midst of you, such as was looked for upwards of 1000 years back, which is now happily discovered in PACKWOOD'S new-invented superior Razor Strop, which will positively take notches from razors, penknives, surgeons' instruments etc., but more particularly adapted to give a delectable smooth edge to an instrument to shave yourself with that ease as is not to be described.
Sold for 3/6, 5/- and 10/6 each.

R. Lyons OPTICIAN, late from Norwich, Respectfully acquaints the Ladies and Gentlemen of Ipswich and its vicinity, that he has taken part of the house and shop of Mr. Simpson, carpenter, in Tavern-street opposite the White Hart Lane, where he will commence business on Monday, 12, November. He makes and sells all sorts of Spectacles, Prospect, Reading and Opera Glasses; Telescopes and Microscopes; Preservers for Young Ladies' and Gentlemen's eyes, particularly those who never used glasses before; Concave and Convex Glasses for short sighted Persons. Ladies and Gentlemen residing in the country, may be suited by sending their Age, or old Glasses. R.L. flatters himself that, from the long experience he has had, in optics, that he can suit the sight equal to any optician in the kingdom. N.B. A variety of gold watches, jewellery, trinkets etc, on reasonable terms.

On Wednesday next will be published Price Three Shillings A concise Treatise on the Progress of Medicine since the year 1753, by W.H. Williams, M.B. F.L.S.
Of Gonville and Caius College, Cambridge, Physician to the Ipswich Dispensary and Laying-in Charity.
Also by the same Author
Hints on the Ventilation of Army Hospitals, and on Regimental Practice. Price 2/-.

Dr. Brodum's Botanical Syrup and Nervous Cordial.
This day is published, price 3/6 a new edition of a Guide to Old Age: or A cure for the Indiscretions of Youth; wherein are laid down the means to obtain a radical cure for nervous, hypochondriac, and consumptive complaints etc. with an Essay on Venereal Complaints, Gleets and Seminal Weaknesses. Neither single, nor married of both sexes should be a moment without having this publication in their possession. The Botanical Syrup is a sovereign remedy against ulcers and many

desperate cases of evil, scurvy and leprosy, as well as in removing pimpled faces, sore legs and other disagreeable erup-
tions the bad effect of taking mercury in.

NEW MUSIC THIS DAY IS PUBLISHED
The Ipswich Volunteers Slow March, Quick March and Funeral
March. Humbly dedicated to the Officers and Gentlemen of the
Corps.
Composed by S. Ball, Master of the Band.
Set for the Piano Forte; likewise for a full Military Band;
Recommended to Voluntary Regiments in general, as it suits a
small Band as well as a Full Military Band.
Price Two Shillings.
Sold by Broderip & Wilkinson, 13 Haymarket, and by
Mr. Bush & Mr. Raw, Music-sellers, Ipswich.

Will. Dixon, Mill wright, Threshing, Winnowing & Chaff Engine
Manufacturers, Return Thanks to Friends and the Public particularly those who have already employed him in the above
branches; informs the same that he has finished a new CHAFF
ENGINE upon a quite new and improved principle, which
when properly loaded will cut with great ease one bushel of
chaff in two minutes or 50 bushels per hour. Gentlemen
Farmers and Millers who wish to favour him with their orders
may depend of having their work well executed and upon the
newest and most improved principles.

Run away, last night, my wife, Bridget Coole, she is a tight
neat body, and has lost one leg: she was seen riding behind
the Priest of the parish through Fermoy, and as we was never
married, I will pay no debts she does not contract; she lisps
with one tooth, and is always talking about fairies and is of
no use but to the owner.
(Reprinted from the Clonnel Journal.)

"Of the uncertainties of our present state, the most dreadful and alarming is the uncertain continuance of Reason." Rasselas.

LODDON ASYLUM — FOR THE RECEPTION OF LUNATICS — NORFOLK

Mr. Guyton Jollye, Surgeon, grateful for the confidence reposed in him by the friends of the many unfortunate persons now under his care, will use his utmost endeavours towards rendering all such comfortable consistent with their cases.

Patients will be received, and humanely taken care of, upon terms agreeable to their circumstances and the accommodation required. The apartments, and the pleasure grounds adjoining the Asylum, may be seen any day, P.M. by Parents and guardians of the insane persons.

SOLOMON'S GUIDE to HEALTH or Advice to both Sexes in a variety of complaints, explaining in a concise and plain manner, the mode, treatment and most efficacious remedies for the following diseases;

Abortion or Miscarriage	Indisposition attendant on
Asthma	Pregnancy
Appetite (loss of)	Indigestion
Barrenness	Juvenile Indiscretion
Bilious Complaints	Lowness of Spirits
Chlorosis or Green Sickness	Menstrual Evacuations
Child Bearing	Nervous Diseases
Fits	Pregnancy
Fluorthibus or Whitges	Phthisis or Cough
Flatulence or Wind	Rheumatism
Gleets	Scrofula
Gonorrhoea	Seminal Weaknesses
Hypochondria or	Scurvy
Melancholy Complaints	Turn of Life etc.

The whole illustrated and interspersed with a variety of authentic facts never before published.

300 pages 3/-

J.T. Allcock — Printer, Bookseller, Bookbinder & Stationer, In the Thoroughfare, Halesworth.
Respectfully informs his Friends and the Public that he has taken possession of the shop and premises of the late Mr. Wm. Gilbert, where he intends carrying on the above branches and hopes, by strict assiduity and attention, to merit their patronage and support.
A CIRCULATING LIBRARY
The most approved Patent Medicines
Catalogues, handbills, club articles, cards etc. printed at the shortest notice on the lowest terms.
Schools supplied and country shops served with goods of the very best quality, on the lowest terms.

Christmas Presents.
Messrs Roberts, Thompson & Co. return their sincere thanks to the public for the very liberal patronage afforded to their various Coach concerns and anxious that Game, Poultry etc. intended for the approaching Christmas should be safely delivered, particularly request their friends will place one full direction *inside* and another *outside* every basket, hamper or other package, and that two full directions on parchment, or strong card be affixed to every loose hare, goose, turkey etc.
R.T. & Co. need hardly observe, that owing to the great quantity of such articles sent by coaches and the uncertain state of the weather at this season of the year, such precaution is absolutely necessary.

SUFFOLK & GENERAL COUNTRY FIRE INSURANCE
Common 2/-   Hazardous 3/-   Farming Stock & Utensils 2/6.

Artificial Teeth with the Enamel, neatly set;
Natural ones engrafted on old stumps, and all other operations which the teeth require, with a perfect cure of all disorders in the gums.

Notes

Abstergent A cleansing agent, used in advertisements to describe laxatives or purgatives.

Accompt To number or account. The archaic form is retained in the word Comptroller. Chaucer was Comptroller of Customs in the 14th century. In the 1950s most large firms had their accounting carried out on 'Comptometers'.

Analeptic A restorative or strengthening medicine — a tonic. Often contained antimony. Dr. James's Fever Powders were very widely used. At the onset of George III's period of insanity in 1788, Dr. James's Powders were prescribed.

Antimonials Medicines containing antimony, a brittle metallic substance, used as an emetic to cause vomiting.

Azotic The old name for nitrogen gas, the fumes of which are deadly.

Bat-Horses Animals used solely for the purpose of transporting an Army officer's equipment. The soldier who had charge of this was a 'Batman'.

Bathing-Season During the 18th century the Medical profession had discovered the health giving properties of sea air and sea bathing, which began the custom of seaside holidays and the development of the various resorts. Although the Prince of Wales favoured Brighton, it was Weymouth, popularised by George III and his family, that was considered as the fashionable place for the young of the period. In Jane Austen's *Emma*, Frank Churchill had become secretly engaged to Jane Fairfax during the Weymouth Season, and at the opening of *Mansfield Park*, Tom Bertram and his friend

Mr. Yates had recently returned from that watering place. Other towns were already achieving a reputation as a family resort; Mr. & Mrs. John Knightley in *Emma* had taken their summer holiday at Southend, where the air was said to have greatly improved their daughter's resistance to sore throats. Mr. Woodhouse, representing the conservative attitude to a new fashion, disliked the idea of Southend but, since his doctor supported the practice of visiting the seaside, he was prepared to endorse his recommendation of Cromer.

Beckwith   John Christmas. 1750-1809
A native of Norwich, he became, after his studies at Oxford, organist at St. Peter Mancroft and then at the Cathedral of Norwich. He was considered to be the highest ranking organist of his day, so the concert at which he was to perform would command a large and fashionable audience.

Boulting-Mill   To boult is to sift. Boulting is a stage in the milling process when the flour is sifted. In *The Trumpet Major* Mrs. Garland and Ann who lived in one half of the Mill House, always knew when 'boulting' was taking place, because a thin film of flour managed to seep through every nook and cranny to deposit a fine layer of white dust on all the furniture.

Boulton   Matthew. 1728-1809.
Followed his father into his Birmingham business as a silver stamper and piercer. Was very successful, opened the Soho Works, and took James Watt into partnership when the latter was looking for assistance to develop his steam engine. He was responsible for

providing coins for the East India Company and the Colonies. In 1797 he produced the first British copper coins, the large, heavy pennies which doubled as 1 oz. weights.

Calomel   Mercurious chloride, used as a purgative; also known as horn quicksilver.

Carter   Thomas. 1735-1804
'C.T.' Carter was born in Dublin. He showed musical promise at an early age, and under the patronage of the Earl of Inchiquin he was sent to study in Italy. From there he went to India where he was for some time the musical director of the Calcutta Theatre. Returning to England, he settled in London, where, in 1775 his musical setting of Bates' *Rival Candidates* at the Drury Lane Theatre was the start of a series of such works. The Dictionary of National Biography dismisses this story of the bogus Handel MS. as a fabrication which first appeared in the *Gentlemen's Magazine*.

Cassimere   Thin, fine twilled woollen cloth, much used in men's clothing. Also known as Kerseymere or Cashmere.

Caulkers   The workmen employed in sealing the seams of wooden ships with CAULK, that is, a mixture of oakum and pitch. Oakum was the fibre unpicked from old ropes. Picking oakum was a task frequently assigned to prisoners or the inmates of Workhouses. You could say that this was an 18th century version of recycling materials.

Chaise   A four-wheeled open carriage with one or two ponies.

Chaldron   A measurement of coal, approx. 36 bushels.

Chalybeate   Mineral or spring water which has been impregnated with iron. As with sea bathing, medical science was claiming curative properties for such wells and springs, and many towns, during the latter half of the 18th century, tried to have a share of the profits being made by those with established 'waters'. At the end of chapter 34 of *The Trumpet Major* Anne Garland comes upon the King, George III and his personal physician who are investigating a sulphurous spring on the outskirts of Budmouth (Weymouth) which was reputed to be producing miraculous cures.

A close look at the drinks department of any supermarket today will reveal a surprising number of bottled mineral waters from all over the British Isles as well as the more famous ones from Europe.

Charity-Children This annual service for the orphan children of London with its impressive procession must have been the inspiration of William Blake's poem 'Holy Thursday' in *Songs of Innocence and Experience.*

Coke Thomas Coke, well known as 'Coke of Norfolk' for his experiments in agriculture.

The silver vase presented to him by the farmers of Norfolk is still in the possession of the family, but the manuscripts have passed to the nation in lieu of taxes and are now in the Bodleian Library, Oxford.

Cooke George Frederick. 1756-1812.

He was considered to be a very fine actor, especially in Shakespearean roles, but his heavy drinking finally ruined his career.

Costiveness Constipation. The people of the period seem to have suffered greatly in this direction. Nowadays we would suggest taking more fibre in the general diet!

Dancing-Masters

Dancing was not only very popular as all the novels of the period show, but was also considered to be an essential part of the education of a young lady. Many dancing-masters travelled great distances to give lessons either at private schools or in large country houses. The master usually accompanied the dancing on a miniature violin.

Dioastrodoxon

A model representing the motion of the planets around the sun. Also known as ORRERY, after Charles Boyle, Earl of Orrey for whom it was made.

Dollars

There was a severe shortage of coins at the end of the 18th century, mainly because of the high price of both gold and silver. It is possible, and several newspaper items bear this out, that fear of invasion caused many people to hide their savings, thus withdrawing even more coins from circulation. In 1797 Spanish dollars were countermarked with the head of George III and came into general circulation. Matthew Boulton was responsible for this work.

The dollar was worth five shillings (25 pence). Cockney slang retained the use of dollar and half dollar (2/6) certainly up to the introduction of metric currency in 1971.

Eager

John. 1782-1853.
Like Beckwith, he was born in Norwich and also became an organist.
He was a page at Knowle to the Duke of Dorset until his patron's insanity led him to run away. He settled in Yarmouth where he made a living as a music teacher. In 1803 he was appointed as Organist to the Corporation of Yarmouth.

He opened a Musical Academy in the Assembly Rooms in Norwich where he expounded his theories on how the performer's hands should be held when playing the pianoforte.

Febrifuge   A cooling medicine used for feverish conditions.

Fillagree   Filigree/Filagree — a type of embroidery using fine gold and silver thread and beads.

Garrard   George. 1760-1826. A painter and sculptor who specialised in animal portraiture. He was elected an Associate of the Royal Academy in 1800.

Greensickness   Anaemia or Chlorosis.

Gutta-Serena   Amaurosis, the partial or total loss of sight caused by the disease of the optic nerve.

Hawkesworth   This story of Keeper Hawkesworth and his miserliness could well have been the basis for Hardy's old Squire Derriman in *The Trumpet Major.*

Hats   *Beaver* — those made of beaver fur.

Chip — made from thin strips of wood woven in the same fashion as those made of STRAW.

Livery — specially made serviceable headwear for servants.

Herberden   Doctor. He had been one of the medical practitioners called in by Sir George Baker to see the king (Geo. III) when he suffered his acute bout of insanity in 1788.

Hypochondria   A term we tend to use in a derogatory sense, but was obviously accepted in those days as a recognised state of mind. Once one accepts this as part of life in the 18th & 19th century, then Mr. Woodhouse in *Emma* becomes more tolerable.

The dictionary definition of 'morbid state of depression due to unnecessary anxiety about health' may not be exact but there is much emphasis on healthy living. Mr. Woodhouse's concern that his lady guests should not eat rich food, is no more comic than the hostess of today who serves only whole foods. His suggestion that the ladies should eat soft boiled eggs would, alas, now be greatly out of favour!

Incledon   Charles. 1763-1826.

He received early choral training at the Exeter Cathedral School. Later he ran away to sea where his musical talents were noticed by his officers who encouraged him to leave the navy and try the stage. He had a fine tenor voice and performed in many operas, although he was considered an unskilful actor. He was reputed to have a bad memory, and a vulgar accent which made him not wholly acceptable in polite society.

Jalop   A purgative drug obtained from the resin contained in the tuberous roots of a Mexican climbing plant. Also used as a verb, to jalop = to purge.

The word survives today in the colloquial 'doctor's jollop' for a bottle of medicine.

Kemble   Charles. 1775-1854.

The Kembles were a theatrical family. Sarah Kemble became Mrs. Siddons.

Charles, although thought to have an ungainly figure, was a very versatile actor.

Livery   Clothes supplied by an employer. Sometimes a specific uniform or colour was worn by all the household servants, but most often the employer was simply responsible for providing his workmen with suitable clothing, as nowadays some employers provide overalls or other forms of protective clothing.

Militia Briefly, the Militia was a Volunteer Reserve Army. The Lord Lieutenant of each county was responsible for mustering the force which with a certain amount of annual training would be prepared to defend the country in the event of an invasion. Able bodied men who had avoided conscription to the regular army had to show that they belonged to the Militia. Although meant to be a volunteer service, conscription became necessary in some areas, but a man was free to make private arrangements for someone else to do his service for him.

Those who have laughed at the makeshift methods employed in the T.V. comedy *Dad's Army*, might enjoy reading how it was when 'Boney' was expected in *The Trumpet Major*.

Opodeldoc Originally a medical plaster. Soap liniments made from a solution of soap in alcohol with camphor, oils of origanum (wild marjoram) rosemary, Pennyroyal, etc.

Orchestrina An elaborate kind of barrel organ intended to give an orchestra-like effect.

Ordinary A public meal provided at a fixed time and price in an inn or eating-house.

Orrey A clockwork model of the planetary system made for the Earl of Orrery by George Graham, a clockmaker, in 1710.

Pelisse Full length woman's cloak with armholes or sleeves.

Pelisses enjoyed a period of high fashion and many ladies in novels and plays of the period concerned themselves over which pelisse they should wear for a certain event.

Phantasmorgaria An exhibition of optical illusions produced chiefly by means of the magic lantern. The first exhibition given in London was in 1802.

Piano-Forte   This very popular instrument which had displaced the harpsichord was the wooden framed grand or square instrument. Now that pianos are coming back into fashion it is possible to come upon examples of the square piano. Sometimes in American films set in the mid or late 1800s one can be seen.

It is interesting that the piano could be hired and I cannot help speculating that this is what Frank Churchill did in *Emma,* when the arrival of a piano for Jane Fairfax set all Highbury agog.

Porter   A very dark, bitter beer, not as thick as stout, made from charred malt. It was an accepted part of the daily diet of the working population, even the Workhouses or Houses of Industry allowing two pints daily per head to their inmates. The rise in wholesale price from just under 2d (1p) per pint to almost 2½d was quite considerable.

Preservers   Goggles used to protect the eyes from dust when out riding in a carriage, or from very bright light.

Prospect-Glasses   Telescopes, field glasses. Quizzing glasses — very popular with short-sighted fops and chaperones who wished to have a close-up view of people.

Press   'A hot Press' refers to the intensive activities of the men responsible for recruiting personnel for the Navy. As this extract shows anyone with connections with the sea, in this case lighthouse keepers, was liable to be 'pressed' into service. Again *The Trumpet Major* gives a good description of a Press.

Roscius   A famous Roman actor of the first century B.C. His name was given to any outstanding actor, the title being held during the 18th century by David Garrick. The YOUNG ROSCIUS was William Henry West BETTY, who was born in Shrewsbury in 1791. His early years were spent in Ireland where his father ran a farm and a linen manufactory. From the accounts of the period one is given a fascinating insight into the standards of acting at that time and the behaviour of audiences. But most interesting is the tremendous build-up which preceded his London debut. Nowadays we are very familiar with the power of the media to establish a performer as a 'star', but in 1804 there were only the newspapers and word of mouth to spread the publicity, yet his impact on the London theatre world must have been similar to that of the first Rock and Roll films shown in the 1950s.

It is interesting to note that one of the plays in his repertoire was *Lovers' Vows*, the play which caused so much anguish to various people in *Mansfield Park*.

Rouleau A coil or roll of material or braided cord, usually gold in colour.

Sale of Wives The practice of wife selling is well documented. One of the best accounts of such dealings is to be found in Hardy's *Mayor of Casterbridge*. Strangely, in that novel, as in this report, it was a sailor who bought the wife, and he took her off to North America, while this real sailor was an American. However, there the similarity ends, Susan Henchard being in no way a termagant.

Scrofula The disease also known as the 'King's Evil' — a chronic enlargement and degeneration of the lymphatic glands.

Seer An Indian measurement — about 2 lbs. in

Se'nnight

weight, or a litre in liquid measure. A corruption of seven-night, that is a week. Although this word is no longer in use, we have retained 'fortnight', that is fourteen-nights or two weeks.

Seven-Shillings

A seemingly odd amount for a coin until one remembers that it was one-third of a guinea, which was twenty-one shillings. In the report of the young woman who stole the baby, it is interesting to note that she gave the child's mother 7/- to buy tea and sugar. This was not just a case of a lady having no small change, but an indication of the high price of the two commodities.

Shew

This form of spelling has now become obsolete, but in Suffolk it has lingered in speech as the past tense of to show. "He shew it to me. . ." is quite common, even among young people, the word rhyming with 'crew'.

Slop Frock

A loose gown or smock worn over wide knickerbockers. Also used as a term to describe cheap ready-made clothes.

Spangles

Originally a small piece of glittering material often inserted into dresses as ornament. The term remains in The Star Spangled Banner of the U.S.A.

Telegraph

A communication system of signals conveyed by upright posts with movable arms which was invented by Chappe in France in 1792.

Tituses

A short, fuzzy haircut.

Velvet

A short, dense, smooth piled material of silk.

Velveteen

A cheaper version of the above using cotton in place of silk.

Wicket

A small gate or door either beside or incorporated within a much larger one. Often to be seen nowadays in large warehouses or at the delivery entrances of large stores.